BOOKS BY

H. Stuart Hughes

AN APPROACH
TO PEACE
AND OTHER ESSAYS

AN APPROACH
TO PEACE

AND OTHER ESSAYS

BY

H. STUART HUGHES

ATHENEUM   NEW YORK

1962

Portions of this book have appeared in *The American Scholar,*
Commentary, Dissent, and *Partisan Review*

TO THE MEMORY OF
FRANZ NEUMANN

Preface

THIS VOLUME is an effort to put together in coherent
order the dissenting opinions on our country's foreign
policy and cultural situation that have been coming to a
boil in the back of my mind for the past ten years. Some
have a measure of emotional detachment; the majority
are frankly polemical. They are intended to stimulate
controversy—to contribute toward awakening the
American people. I fervently hope they will do so.

The six essays in Part I present a single connected
argument—a plea for a radical rethinking of foreign policy assumptions. The essays in the second and third
parts pursue related topics whose relevance to the main
theme should be apparent by the time the reader comes
to the final chapter. Part II assesses the weakening of
ideological commitment in Europe today and its consequences for the political solidarity of the West. Part III
treats of people like myself: American writers and
teachers. Here I contend that we are not living up to
our responsibilities, that we have failed to resist with
enough determination the pressures toward cultural ba-
nality and the threat of thermonuclear war or to think
of the future in a sufficiently radical and utopian fashion. Through this last part of the argument, an evocation of the McCarthy years serves as a constant reminder
of our past weaknesses and future perils.

I first formulated these views on the ideological and cultural dilemmas of the mid-century in a volume entitled *An Essay for Our Times,* originally published in 1950 and now out of print. This little book—written before McCarthy's rise and published, as it happened, just a few days prior to his famous initial speech at Wheeling, West Virginia—anticipated many of the issues that became of burning urgency in the years immediately following and that are still at the center of my concerns. Now, twelve years later, I have a similar sense of attempting *in extremis* to give voice to the common interests of a humanity transcending the barriers drawn by the cold war, before the blight of national and ideological hatred descends on us once again.

In the quarter century that has passed since I came to ideological awareness, I have traversed five successive phases in trying to cope with Soviet and Communist behavior. During the mid-thirties I endorsed the Popular Front idea. After that came four years of growing animosity, starting around 1937, when people like myself awoke to the horror of the great purge, and punctuated by the catastrophe in Spain, the Nazi-Soviet pact, and the winter war in Finland, until in 1941 the German invasion of Russia at length cast the Soviet Union in a more attractive role. The third phase was one of renewed Popular Front—the left-ideological counterpart to the military alliance against Hitler—which was already breaking up in the weeks between the Yalta conference and the end of the European conflict and which had totally expired by 1948. There followed the years of cold war hostility until the death of Stalin in 1953, and, finally, the present phase, whose ultimate outlines are

necessarily unclear, but whose salient characteristics derive from the mitigation of authoritarian rule within the
Soviet Union itself, the emergence of China and the
newly-liberated nations of Asia and Africa, and, most
pervasively, the thermonuclear balance of terror between the Communist and the Western worlds.

During all these phases, I have never remotely
thought of becoming a Communist. My sympathies have
mostly been with democratic socialism—although I have
been subject to disconcerting attacks of conservative
regression—and I have only infrequently found myself
saying something that happened to be the current Communist line. At the same time I have never been a strenuous anti-Communist; even in the periods when I saw
the rulers of the Soviet Union pursuing a particularly
brutal policy—in the late 1930's and again in the last
years of Stalin's tyranny—I have found it difficult to
concentrate my energies against them. I think this is because I have never felt that opposition to Communism
was the main matter at hand; it was always secondary to
some greater battle, and one in which we might well
need the Communists as allies. In the first three phases
of my ideological journey, the enemy was Nazism, which
I continue to regard as almost wholly evil, as opposed to
Communism, in which I discover some potentiality for
good. More recently, the enemy has been the threat of
thermonuclear war itself, and I find it difficult to imagine how one could regard the points at issue between
ourselves and the Russians as overriding our common
interest in preventing a catastrophe beyond repair.

Once again today, as a quarter century ago, when I
was turning twenty, the best chance for the salvation of
humanity lies in an understanding between the Soviet
Union and the democracies of the West. The Popular

Fronts of the mid 1930's, I know, disappointed the
hopes of their Western supporters: they were exploited
by the Communists to sectarian ends. But basically they
were not mistaken. In 1936 there was no *good* course of
action available—just as in 1962, there was only a
choice of evils and of risks. Among the choices offered,
the Popular Front gave the most promise.

It failed because it came too early. Soviet Communism was entering its most ruthless phase, and Stalin
was in charge. With the passage of a quarter century,
both the society and the rulers of the Soviet Union have
changed notably, although most Americans do not yet
realize it. A major purpose of these essays is to help
them to such a realization. And it is accompanied by
the hope that there may emerge a new type of Popular
Front mentality, arising out of a common desire for
peace on both sides of the conventional cold war frontier. In this perspective the original Popular Fronts
would finally figure as what they aspired to be at the
time, the ideological prerequisites for the twentieth-
century humanism of a collectivist society.

Perhaps half the present volume has been previously
published in article form. Chapter 7 appeared in *Dissent,* Chapter 11 in *The American Scholar,* a few para-
graphs of the Preface and of Chapters 3 and 5 in
Partisan Review, and substantial parts of Chapters 1, 2,
4, 8, 9, and 10 in *Commentary,* to whose successive edi-
tors, Martin Greenberg and Norman Podhoretz, I am
particularly grateful for the hospitality and encouragement they have given my writing over the past eight
years. I am indebted to all these journals for their per-
mission to republish. My thanks also go to Hiram

Haydn, of Atheneum, and to Nanette Mengel, who typed the manuscript, for their good-humored confidence in the present work.

One final debt remains—to the friends in whose company a number of these thoughts first came out as conversational exchange. I think especially of Mario Casalini, Fairman C. Cowan, Robert A. Dahl, Karl W. Deutsch, Richard Hofstadter, Arturo Carlo Jemolo, John J. Kapstein, Bernard Léger, Herbert Marcuse, Hans Meyerhoff, Barrington Moore Jr., David Riesman, Bruno Rossi, Carl E. Schorske, Edmund Wilson, and the departed friend to whom the book is dedicated.

Contents

I

AN APPROACH
TO PEACE

CHAPTER 1

A New Start in
Foreign Policy

I THINK it is time to make a new start. It is time to rethink from the beginning the assumptions on which
American foreign policy and nearly all public discussion of that policy are currently based. We need to es-
tablish a new order of priorities and a new hierarchy
of values.

The way to begin is to reverse the usual definition
of our enemy. Day in and day out we are told that
international Communism is the enemy—an enemy so
deadly that we should be willing even to risk thermonuclear warfare to stop its advance. In brief, we are
assured that Communism is worse than war. I suggest
we reverse that order; I suggest that we subscribe instead to Governor Muñoz Marin's argument that war
itself rather than Communism is our number one enemy.[1]

Once we have made this enormous shift in emphasis
—once we have made this conversion from one set of
values to another—all sorts of other matters fall into
line. We have gained intellectual elbow-room. We can

1. Godkin Lecture delivered at Harvard University, April 28,
1959.

begin to think of the cold war in terms of its irreducible
realities rather than in current slogans and stereotypes.
We can start narrowing and defining more precisely the
issues that set us at odds with the Russians and the
Chinese. We can begin to look with new eyes both at
ourselves and at our adversaries.

I believe that most of the polemics of the past twelve
or fifteen years are irrelevant today—that both the
usual anti-Soviet statements and the minority opinions
of the Soviet apologists are equally pointless. I believe
that the United States and the Soviet Union *are* very
different—but not as different as they are popularly
supposed to be. I believe that this difference *is* decisive—but not in the way it is usually expressed. We
have more in common with the Russians than either
side realizes. Above all, we have a common—and overriding—interest in stopping the drift toward thermonuclear warfare before it is too late.

In a whole series of crises over the past few years,
the reaction of the American public has followed a
similar and disquieting pattern. It has oscillated wildly
between extremes, from apathy to near-hysteria; it
has shifted suddenly and violently from rally-round-
the-flag to scuttle-and-run. Such a state of mind is
scarcely conducive to balanced judgments in the realm
of foreign relations. It means that all of us—both
leaders and led—are finding it nearly impossible to
reach a clear-eyed assessment of where we stand. An
alternation between truculence and panic is just about
the worst possible position from which to make the
crucial choices that currently confront us.

Why have we allowed ourselves to drift into so dangerous a pass? I think it is because we have become

the prisoners of our own propaganda. We have come to believe what the public-relations experts have told us —to believe it, that is, until all of a sudden a brutal revelation of the truth has plunged us from euphoria into despair. I doubt whether in the history of modern democracy there has ever been so yawning a gap between the official story and the reality, between public rhetoric and private knowledge. Take the crisis of 1958 over Quemoy (or that over Laos two and a half years later). The official talk was of "holding the line" for the West in Asia; we were handed the threadbare tale of the domino blocks that would all come tumbling down if a single little one were pulled away. The truth of the matter was that there was scarcely any Western line to be held: our European allies were against us; among the Asian nations that backed us, only the Philippines really counted; we were exposed "naked to our enemies" as a rich, pampered country, hated and envied, isolated by our doctrinaire devotion to capitalism in a world of poverty and overpopulation in which single-party, more or less socialist states were rapidly becoming the norm.

In brief, we were perilously overextended. We are still overextended. We have all sorts of commitments and pledges abroad which we have no idea how to honor. We hate to come out and say that we cannot possibly honor them—to do so would be to show "weakness." So our leaders restrict themselves to vague moral assurances, occasionally backed up by still vaguer nuclear threats, which (fortunately) few people, either here or abroad, as yet take very seriously.

What we lack today is leadership prepared to disclose the international facts of life to an American people which has too long been sheltered from them. We need

calm and quiet figures—men with a talent for telling
unpleasant truths in a tone that will forestall both anger
and panic, men equipped to lay bare our illusions, but
gently and humanely. Such men should be without
vulgar ambition and with little regard for popularity,
for surely the task I am suggesting is one of the most
unpopular that an American administration has ever
faced. Today is not a time for "greatness"—at least as
conventionally defined—or for leaders who want to
make a name in history. It is a time for reflection and
compassion.

Since our leaders are failing to do the job, it is up
to some of us private citizens to present an alternative
view of international reality to set against the one
handed down by official spokesmen and by most of the
press. I should like to piece together such a view, in
the form of a rough summary of where we stand today.

Let us start with Europe. Here the basic fact that is
not being made clear to the American public is that
Communism no longer presents the danger that it did
ten or fifteen years ago. Since the *coup d'état* of February, 1948, in Czechoslovakia, international Communism has made no advances *in Europe*. Indeed, it
has retreated in one form or another in at least three
places—Yugoslavia, Austria, and Poland. The two
great Communist parties of France and Italy—the only
two parties of any importance outside the Communist-
dominated countries themselves—are both in a state
of decrepitude. They have kept their massive voting
strength and their ability to insulate their following from
the main course of the national life; but they have
proved unable to mobilize this following for any active
purposes of their own choosing: it has become a frozen,

inert mass—little more. It has lost its head and its heart—most of its leading intellectuals and the moral force that once inspired it to devotion and sacrifice. Of these changed circumstances the Soviet leaders themselves seem to be well aware; their passivity toward the advent of de Gaulle in 1958 suggested a kind of weary defeatism.

Thus the first corollary to a recognition of the decay of Communism in Western and Central Europe is a new look at the German problem. Currently we are stuck fast on the old Adenauer line—the insistence that unification can come only through unfettered elections, with the resulting all-German state free to choose a foreign policy of military alliance with the West. Our government refuses even to discuss the possibility of reuniting the country through a federation of the two existing German states. Perhaps it is too late for such a proposal. Perhaps the chance has passed: what was a realistic possibility five years ago may no longer be open to us. One of the most curious features of the Berlin crisis of 1961 was the way both sides tacitly assumed the permanent division of Germany. From our standpoint, there is economic rationality behind such an assumption: West Germany's membership in the Common Market offers a more convincing argument against close relations with the East than any of the ideological or strategic objections that have been advanced in the past. Perhaps the best we can hope for now is to stabilize the *de facto* situation.

In this context, "stabilize" is the key word. It is an interest that the United States and the Soviet Union share, however much our press may obscure it. In respect to Europe, Russia, like our own country, is a "have" power: it has a stake in the established order.

(Indeed, the Soviet leaders may increasingly become defenders of the *status quo* elsewhere, as competition from the Chinese mounts in intensity.) *They* know that Communism stands little chance in Western Europe; *we* know (although we seldom admit it) that Communism has come to Eastern Europe to stay. Both sides—and the European populations as well—have every reason to favor freezing the situation along the present lines of economic and ideological cleavage.

Beyond that, both of us have an interest in creating a zone of military disengagement or neutralization in Central Europe. This is a possibility that need not invariably be discussed, as it mostly has been in the past, as closely bound up with German reunification; the latter question can wait until opinion both in the East and in the West has become better prepared for it. Nor is neutralization the trap for Western innocents that it is conventionally supposed to be. Here once again we are falling into a line of reasoning that has done us much harm in the past—the notion that our Communist adversaries are infinitely cleverer than we are and that it is always they who will be the gainers in a solution of compromise. Isn't this a game that two can play? And don't we in this particular case hold the stronger cards? Certainly the military neutralization of the two German states would mean for the immediate future the continuance of Communist domination and Communist institutions in the Eastern part. But would this arrangement necessarily be permanent? I do not think so, and I do not believe that the Soviet leaders think so either. Some kind of federation, I believe, would sooner or later result, and in such a relationship the stronger partner is almost bound to achieve predominance. In Germany as it is now constituted, the

Western part has two-thirds of the area, three-quarters of the population, and the bulk of the industrial resources. Eventually such a preponderance could scarcely fail to make itself felt: the pressure of neighboring example would become irresistible. The *economic* structure in the East might remain socialized, but the *political* institutions and practices would begin to evolve in a liberal direction.

The same considerations apply in the more strictly military sphere. Surely the American position in Europe today is such as to make us wonder whether a federated and neutralized Germany might not be a worthwhile exchange for the military ally we now have in its Western part. NATO is barely holding together. One body of Germans remains more than doubtful whether it wants to be armed (or defended by others) with nuclear warheads and guided missiles; the other is regressing toward military nationalism. Beyond that, the American-manned bases in Germany and the increasing probability of West Germany's becoming a nuclear power present the sorest point in our task of convincing the Russians that we have no aggressive intentions toward them. The whole situation is far from promising. With the German military contribution to the Western alliance looking more and more problematical and threatening, the virtues of neutralization are becoming increasingly evident—at the very least a relaxation of international tension and a face-saving fashion of getting ourselves off the hook. In military terms, our own position vis-à-vis *our* part of Germany offers some sobering comparisons with the obvious embarrassment of the Soviet leaders in theirs.

This brings us to the second corollary to the view that Communist expansion no longer offers a clear and present danger in Europe. For more than eight years now—ever since the death of Stalin—such a view has been gaining among well-informed Europeans. And they have been drawing the conclusion from it that their military arrangements with the United States no longer make sense. Quite obviously, they reason, the really vulnerable and tempting regions for the expansion of Communist influence lie outside Europe and are likely to remain extra-European for a long time to come. From 1948 to 1953 the prime target was East Asia; subsequently it was the Near East; today the future areas of ideological exploitation are opening up in Africa and Latin America. Most of the time Europe is simply being bypassed. Except for the issue of Germany—where there exist real possibilities for a solution satisfactory to both sides—the great decisions in the struggle of the superpowers are being taken elsewhere in the world. The prospect is a novel one for Europeans: it involves a thorough refocusing of their traditional view of their own continent as the center of the universe. Yet once this psychological adjustment is made, the vista it opens up is intoxicating in the extreme—that is, an outside chance for immunity from the major power struggle. And in this perspective, the presence of American troops in Central Europe looks less like a welcome defense than like an egregious provocation to Soviet attack.

It is no wonder, then, that "neutralism" of all varieties has gained so many adherents in the past decade. Soon it may be the dominant mentality on the European Continent, and even—in a modified, Commonwealth-oriented form—in Britain also. Conventionally, such a prospect fills American policy makers with dread: it conjures up the specter of a nation without friends. But this is to take a superficial and narrowly military view of the matter. In a neutralized Europe—as with the more immediate prospect of an uncommitted Germany—the decision to remain detached from the cold warfare of the superpowers would be no more than formal. It would constitute an undertaking on the part of the Europeans to do nothing that might deepen the present international cleavage and, perhaps, from time to time a more positive effort to reduce Soviet-American hostility. But it would not imply any commitment to refrain from expressions of sympathy or solidarity with one side or the other. Obviously this latter would be impossible: it was the great illusion of President Wilson that he could enjoin such a course on his countrymen in the opening years of the First World War. In the cultural and ideological sense, the vast majority of Europeans naturally feel closer links with the United States than with the Soviet Union. Indeed, in many cases it has been only the unpopularity of the military tie with our country that has held back this pro-American feeling from heartfelt expression.

If all the foregoing is true, one further element needs to be added. For the past eight years—again, since the death of Stalin and the settlement of the Korean and Indochinese wars—the Communist camp has made its spectacular (and extra-European) gains less through military action than through economic and cultural penetration. And such appears to be the prospect for the future, despite the alarms over individual areas of local warfare. When the chances for peaceful penetration are so enticing, it seems fantastic to suppose that the leaders of the Soviet Union would imperil them by a reckless resort to armed attack. A continuation of the trend of the last decade seems the most likely—

that is, an international ideological competition in which trade missions, technical experts, and artists on tour offer just as persuasive weapons as shipments of tanks and planes. And in competition of this sort, a generalized sympathy on the part of peoples and governments is far more to be desired than a military alliance resting on sullen acceptance.

So much for Europe. Yet if a drastic reduction in the military emphasis of American policy makes sense here, how much more is this the case in the underdeveloped areas of Asia and Africa. If NATO is rickety, surely SEATO and CENTO are just about worthless. When we ask ourselves why our country has failed so notably in these latter alliances in non-European parts of the world, the simple answer is that we have taken the wrong actions *most* of the time and explained these actions in the wrong terms nearly *all* the time.

I have said earlier that in Asia and Africa single-party, more or less socialist states are rapidly becoming the norm. Toward societies of this kind the Soviet Union finds itself in a more favorable position than do we in the competitive proffering of aid and advice. The Russians can exploit the undeniable attraction of their own planned economy and, with it, their ability to channel foreign aid in directions of their own choosing —that is, in most cases, where the propaganda effect will be greatest. For our part, we are stuck with the rhetoric of "free enterprise"—a slogan to which we cling more dogmatically in the foreign field than in our current practice at home. It is in this respect in particular that we have shown the most devastating lack of imagination in our dealings with Asian and African nations: to Americans, "free enterprise" has a ring of generosity and sturdy individualism; for newly liberated colonials, it strikes a hollow note of exploitation, economic waste, and solidarity with native profiteers.

In the same fashion, a Soviet engineer or agronomist who is used to rough living and is not reluctant to get his hands dirty in the back country makes a better impression than his American opposite number who is dependent on his luxuries and spends most of his time in urban centers. And in this connection there has arisen one of the most baffling of the paradoxes in which our economic relations abroad have become entangled. We think of ourselves as an idealistic people, and of the Russians as godless materialists; yet the image of ourselves we project overseas is of a goods-oriented society wallowing in luxury. In contrast, the Russians present the picture of a certain Spartan virtue and of a society whose economic level is sufficiently above that of its impoverished neighbors to serve as a guideline but not (like our own) so far removed as to seem alien and impossible of attainment. To a people such as the Indians, committed by philosophical tradition to the "nonmaterial," Soviet society, for all its despotism and cruelty, has attractions that American society cannot match. And not the least of these is the visible demonstration it offers of how an agrarian economy can industrialize itself by its unaided efforts in a matter of two generations.

Does this mean that there is nothing we can do, that the Soviet Union has all the advantages in competing for the friendship of the newly liberated, the uncommitted, and the underdeveloped nations of the earth? Of course not. If we begin to put forward our true ideological assets, rather than persisting in hiding them from foreign view, there is a good chance that we can reverse the present trend before it is too late.

In this regard, I agree totally with C. Wright Mills that American capitalism is not "an exportable system." [2] Until we put such a conviction in the very center of our foreign dealings, our policy will continue to be what it is today—timid, halting, and unattractive. Once we make this basic shift, however, all sorts of now unexpected possibilities will open up. For then we can begin to project abroad the more appealing features of our own society, the aspects that we are well aware of at home but fail to talk about overseas. We can begin to demonstrate the vast changes in our practices and attitudes that have come about in the past generation—the discrediting of the philosophy of relentless acquisition, the acceptance of the welfare state, the cult of gentleness and tolerance in personal and intergroup relations. We can begin to suggest that as a hard-working, *noncompetitive* society we have newly acquired virtues of our own, whose very existence most foreigners scarcely suspect. In brief, we can offer the image of a nation steering its patient, expert, pragmatic way between the completely planned and the ruthlessly competitive, a nation ready to judge the practices of its potential friends with similar open-mindedness.

In this one respect, at least, the Kennedy administration has made a real change. It has grasped the simple fact that if newly liberated nations want their *state* development plans underwritten with money and technical help, there is no earthly reason, aside from doctrinaire devotion to "free enterprise," why we should not do just that. The President and his advisers have also begun to show an awareness that the reward for such generosity will only rarely be a military alliance

2. *The Causes of World War Three* (New York: Simon and Schuster, Inc., 1958), p. 72.

or a pledge of undying friendship. That is not at all what the leaders of the formerly colonial peoples and of those about to attain independence have in mind. For them freedom from commitment in the struggle of the superpowers ranks as a first necessity. They refuse to choose sides—they are not interested in all-or-nothing choices of any sort. They are groping in a highly tentative fashion to define what comes next after the attainment of national independence. And in this search they are thoroughly eclectic about adopting apparently incompatible practices from *both* the major ideological contestants.

At the same time, their policy follows a quite coherent logic of its own. And it is in our failure to realize this fact that we have made our fundamental error in dealing with the underdeveloped areas of Asia, Africa, and Latin America. We have insisted on regarding their problems as a function of our own struggle with Communism and the Soviet Union. A moment's reflection will suggest how wrong this reasoning has been. The problems of the former European colonies —of "backward" peoples newly raised to nationhood— have only a peripheral connection with Communism and Soviet expansion. They would have existed in any case, even if no Bolshevik Revolution had occurred and no Communist International been launched. The process of liberation might have been less precipitate, but sooner or later it would have come about just the same. And after liberation, the problems of economic development, of markets for staple crops, of literacy and hygiene would have appeared exactly as they are manifest today—and far overshadowing the doctrinal question of ideological choice. The convergence of Communism with colonial liberation has given the latter process its explosive force; but it has not changed its long-range fundamentals.

So we reach the end point of the present analysis: in respect to what most of the world's people care most about, the ideological and great power struggle between the Soviet Union and the United States is *supremely irrelevant.* In our overwhelmingly military emphasis overseas we have neglected what is really important and have gotten ourselves into all sorts of impossible dilemmas, where no conceivable advantage can be obtained. We have fallen into the opposite extreme from the isolationist mentality that was once our undoing. Where formerly we did too little in the foreign sphere, we have now been doing too much. A secretary of state like John Foster Dulles became a general busybody, always ready to set forth on his Sisyphean labors of propping up and plastering over. It never seemed to occur to him that some of the ills toward which he rushed off to apply his questionable nostrums were by their very nature incurable. The idea apparently never dawned on him that certain situations simply had to be let alone—that there were some places where no visible American interest was at stake and where the only sensible policy was to "sit this one out."

More and more, it seems to me, an attitude of benevolent detachment, always alert to help where help is needed *and asked for,* but never importunate or intruding, should be the guiding principle of American policy toward the fast-growing segment of mankind that chooses to remain neutral in the power struggle.

If our situation is indeed as I have described it, then nearly all the talk that has gone on during the past decade about "roll-back" or the "liberation" of Com-

munist countries is patently absurd. And even the notion of "holding a line"—except in a few favored areas
of well-established democracy or near-democracy—is
almost equally beside the point. We shall not begin to
reach a realistic judgment of foreign policy alternatives
until we recognize that matters are going to get worse
for us before they get better. Several more areas are
likely to "go Communist" (or something close to it)
before the tide starts to run in another direction.

Such has long been the unstated major premise of
Britain's foreign policy. The British have apparently
been convinced that the Atlantic powers are forced by
circumstances to fight what is little more than a delay-
ing action, that the battles that have been lost—China,
Indochina, and the rest—are simply the first of a series of probable defeats that will end only when the
Communist world has become so vastly extended as to
prove unmanageable, or until some notable change of
heart takes place within the Communist governing class.
Under these circumstances, the British have tried to
play a weak hand with some sort of style—to put a
good face on concessions they have resisted up to the
last possible moment; to accept diplomatic humiliation
in return for a window or two on the East; and to
work quietly and tirelessly to widen every possible
crevice in the apparently monolithic international
alignment confronting them. This Fabian policy has
certainly been inglorious.[3] It has no triumphs to show
—only the accidental vindication of the Titoist defec-
tion from the Communist camp. Yet without assuming some such basic premise, it is impossible to under-

3. Britain's attack on Suez in 1956 was an obvious exception
to such a policy line, and its very uncharacteristic quality was
one reason for its failure.

stand the equanimity with which the British accepted
the victory of Mao Tse-tung in China and the neutralist
course of Nehru in India.

This is not to say that the British have been pleased
by what has happened in Asia during the past two
decades. But the comparatively elegant fashion in
which they departed from India and the sudden en-
hancement of their standing among Asians that resulted from it have given them a serenity in dealing with Far Eastern problems that has contrasted
markedly with the more harassed attitude of the French
and Americans. The Indochinese war is a case in point.
The tragic confusion in its conduct and the Franco-
American misunderstandings that punctuated it arose
from the fact that it simultaneously formed part of the
world-wide struggle against Communist expansion and
was a thoroughly anachronistic effort to hold on to the
last important European colony in Asia. Up to the very
end, these two elements were never properly disen-
tangled. Apparently the British realized this all along:
enlightened by their experience in India, they suspected
that the Indochinese war could never be brought to a
satisfactory conclusion. Similarly, their attitude of detachment with regard to neutralism and Communist in-
filtration in Southeast Asia suggests a conviction that
the Western powers can do little to influence the internal evolution of that area. A corresponding skepticism extends to the efforts of American policy makers
to maintain an Asian anti-Communist front out of what
to the British seem little more than bits and pieces—
Pakistan, Thailand, the Philippines, and Formosa. The
British attitude has the virtues and the weaknesses of
the wisdom of the disabused.

Nothing could be farther from the conventional

American insistence on positive solutions. Yet I am suggesting that we can profit by British experience and example in reevaluating our own foreign policy. I know the answer I will receive: "Munich"—with all its overtones of suspicion of British moral feebleness. The comparison with Munich is bound to come up in any policy discussion that smacks of defeatism or strategic withdrawal. And quite legitimately so: the historical parallel with the present is so obvious that it can not (and should not) be evaded. Anyone who proposes views such as mine can hardly expect to be taken seriously unless he makes a conscientious effort to deal with the Munich precedent.

Granted all that, I think that Munich offers a false analogy. "Appeasement" was not originally an evil word, and a policy that is folly in one context may be simple common sense in another. The world outlook today is totally different from what it was in 1938; it is only superficially that circumstances seem alike. In the 1930's we were dealing with Nazism—a negative force of hatred and destruction, whose "demonic" nature sharply limited its attraction beyond the areas of German speech and sympathy. Today we face Communism —a positive force of social and economic reconstruction with a profound appeal to more than half the population of the world, a movement which, despite all the terror and perversion of ideals with which it is associated, has its origins and ultimate aspirations in the major Western tradition of reason and humanity. Nazism was a temporary aberration of the European spirit; Communism seems likely to remain a permanent (and growing) feature of the ideological landscape as long as anyone now living remains on earth.

Yet—I can hear the objections now—what is all this

but "wave of the future" reasoning, a vulgar "histori-
cist" argument too shoddy to be tolerated even for an
instant? If what I am saying were only that, my readers
would be quite right to be impatient with me. But
there is more to it than an argument from long-range
historical trends. There is the whole question of weaponry and the attitude toward warfare of the authoritarian system in question. The Nazi Reich was dedicated
to armed combat; Hitler *wanted* war and felt de-
frauded when the Munich settlement robbed him of it.
Communism—both in theory and in practice—regards
war only as a last resort.[4]

Moreover, in the quarter century that has passed
since Munich, the weapons situation has changed totally. The defeat of Nazi power in war—and with it
the destruction of fascism throughout Europe—was a
technically feasible operation. And the Second World
War did accomplish just that. In terms of realistic calculation, the conflict made sense—the gains exceeded
the losses. In moral terms also, the war was justifiable:
the suffering it inflicted was commensurate with the
evil to be eradicated; in its early stages, at least, it
conformed to the traditional ethical and theological
definitions of a "just" war.[5] It is significant that those
who fought and won the Second World War still regard
it as such; they do not regret what they did. As opposed to the chorus of self-reproach that began among
the victors even before the Treaty of Versailles had
been signed, no such wave of "revisionism" as followed
the First World War has succeeded to the Second.
Seventeen years have passed, and still no apologies
are being offered.

4. See George F. Kennan, *Russia and the West Under Lenin
and Stalin* (Boston: Little, Brown & Company, 1961), p. 389.
   5. For further comment on this point, see Chapter 4.

I hardly need add that none of the above considerations applies today. A feasible war, a just war, the destruction in battle of Communist "evil"—all this is no more than fantasy, but a fantasy laden with peril to the human race. A generation ago, it was possible to think of settling accounts with Hitler while the majority of mankind stood by and watched. Today this possibility no longer exists; we are all threatened together by the same weapons of mass destruction. The final and clinching argument against the analogy from Munich to the present is the attitude of the spectators on the sidelines. In 1938 and 1939 these applauded, or at least regarded with a benevolent detachment, the idea of a showdown with Hitler. Today the billion-odd citizens of the still underdeveloped and still uncommitted world would vehemently oppose a similar reckoning with Communism, no matter what suffering and what denial of liberty life under Communist rule might entail.

Analogies from the past, then, will not do. We are obliged to think for ourselves now, without help from our predecessors or the crusading days of our own youth. The circumstances are unprecedented; so must our thinking be also. As every creative scientist knows, the only way an apparently insoluble problem can be approached is by entertaining all possible hypotheses, however wild they may at first appear. That is what I propose to do in these essays. My standpoint will be frankly radical and unashamedly utopian. For I agree with Mills that "We are at a curious juncture in the history of human insanity; in the name of realism, men are quite mad, and precisely what they call utopian is now the condition of human survival." [6]

6. *Causes of World War Three*, p. 113.

CHAPTER 2

. . . To Fit Our Cloth

ONE OF THE deepest of the many obscurities in the understanding of history surrounds the problem of how and when large numbers of people change their minds. Again and again in our studies we historians are confronted by a situation that seems to defy explanation in the terms to which we are accustomed—a sudden shift of mass emotion, a new enthusiasm that has swept through an entire community, or the equally unanticipated collapse of some popular credence—events such as these fly in the face of our most cherished prejudices. We have been trained to think of history in terms of slow change and gradual development. We are at a loss to account for the sudden and the catastrophic.

In my own case—as, I judge, in that of many other teachers of history—a reading of *War and Peace* first opened my eyes to a more satisfactory understanding of the past. One of the great merits of Tolstoi's novel is that it conveys a sense of events as actually in the process of occurring. As conventionally written and taught, history is too orderly: the historian knows the outcome, and this knowledge infuses his account with a quality of inevitability to which the participants in the events themselves were total strangers. In *War and Peace* the full disorder of actual occurrence is restored to history; with a disarming innocence of manner, the author leads his reader into the very center of events, until the reader quite unexpectedly finds himself caught up in the doubts and fears of the historical actors.

It is Tolstoi's picture of General Kutusov at the Battle of Borodino that conveys most arrestingly what I have in mind. Kutusov, we may recall, is far from being in control of events. He knows this—yet at the same time he knows that it is expected of him that he appear to be in control. It is up to him to incarnate the conviction of the Russian people that the French invaders will be repulsed and ultimately expelled from the country. Kutusov does not quite know how this is to be done—his mind is shrewd, but imprecise and slow-moving—yet he shares the popular conviction that it will in some fashion be accomplished. He also knows that a battle is expected of him, although he is quite sure that a battle will settle nothing, that it will only be useless slaughter. But a battle before Moscow is essential to the popular faith. Hence he sits—massive, imperturbable, apparently half-asleep—overlooking the field of Borodino, simply *representing* in admirably tangible fashion the unshakable conviction of his people, ostensibly directing a battle which, like the wider course of the war itself, is quite beyond his control.

Why, then, does he sit so stolid in his confidence? Because at some point in the past weeks it has dawned on him that time is on his side. Vaguely, gropingly, like the soldiers and peasants who trust in him, he has arrived at the belief that Napoleon can be stopped. The exact outlines of the future are still impenetrable. But the final result can each day be more clearly discerned. And on the other side, in the ranks of the Em-

peror's Grand Army, there are manifest the beginnings
of panic—of a loss of confidence that will soon become
a rout.

This passage from hope to despair, or from fear to
confidence, is what the physiologists or psychologists
would call crossing a threshold. It is a process com-
pounded of countless individual alterations in sentiment
that are too minute for the historian to trace. Their
sum, however, amounts to a psychological revolution.
These gusts and shifts of popular emotion are obviously not as sudden as they seem. They are prepared
over long periods and by subterranean processes at
which we can do little more than guess. But when the
change *does* appear on the surface, it comes with a
rush. Like Montaigne's peasant girl who found that she
could no longer perform her morning routine of lifting her pet calf, the change may well appear from one
day to the next, almost without warning, and totally
disproportionate to its apparent "cause."

The decisive feature of such a change is this: as opposed to the more usual alterations in opinion of which
we read in our daily newspaper, it involves the passive
and inarticulate majority of society. It spreads beyond
the ranks of the articulate and the politically committed
to affect the opinion of those who scarcely know what
their own sentiments are. One fine morning the man
totally uninterested in public affairs unexpectedly wakes
up to a new conviction.

It was one of these enormous changes that took
place in American and world opinion when the Russians launched their Sputnik in the autumn of 1957.
Half a decade has passed since then, and still our
leaders have not drawn the consequences—for our own

country, for our allies, and for the uncommitted nations
of the world.

Without some such hypothesis about how large
masses of people lose an old conviction or reach a new
one, we should be at a loss to account for the great and
permanent alterations of sentiment in our common
past. We should not be able to understand, for example, how rather suddenly in the middle of the seven-
teenth century religion came to seem a matter no longer
worth fighting over, and the religious boundaries of
Europe settled down to the outlines that have remained
virtually unchanged until this day. Similarly, we should
be in no position to assess those curious and recurring
situations in which a war has gone on so long that the
antagonists have almost forgotten their original aims—
the situation, depicted by Jonathan Swift in his *Conduct of the Allies,* of a coalition that has in effect accomplished what it set out to do and now is held together by no more than a habit of warfare in common;
in such circumstances, almost overnight the popular
pressure for an immediate peace may become overwhelming.

By the same process, and closer to our own time, we
are just beginning to understand—or rather, we are
beginning to revive our understanding—of the mentality that was responsible for the Munich pact of 1938.
Once again, it was hindsight that for nearly two decades made the motives of the men of Munich incomprehensible to us. In the light of the war that followed,
the conduct of such leaders as Chamberlain and Daladier seemed merely fatuous. Today we are in a better
position to appreciate the problem they faced. Once

more we can understand the mentality of peace at any price. For what a number of Western statesmen and publicists have been telling us during the past half decade comes very close to just that. In more acceptable terminology, perhaps, they have declared that war is "unthinkable" under present circumstances of anticipated mutual destruction. When one says that war is "unthinkable," one means quite literally that one is unwilling to think about it. The alternative to peace has been foreclosed.

In 1938, also, war for the Western democracies was unthinkable. Chamberlain and Daladier knew it; they judged their own peoples correctly, and acted accordingly. The difference between the two was simply this: Chamberlain had illusions about the future, and Daladier had none. The latter knew that the war would eventually have to be fought—but he also knew that this was morally impossible so long as the inarticulate mass of the French people was unprepared to accept the idea. A year later, he saw no alternative to taking the plunge—but his people were still unready. The decisive difference between the war efforts of the French and of the British in the first phase of the conflict was that the latter had time to wake up to the psychological necessities of warfare, while the former were overwhelmed before they were really awake. In the sense of a profound moral shift, the Second World War did not begin for the Western democracies in September, 1939, but nine months later, when the British found themselves standing alone.

It may be painful for us to recognize—yet it is imperative that we do so if we are to face our future with a minimum of mental clarity—that the past few years have witnessed a profound psychological change in the *opposite direction* from what occurred in Britain and what began to occur in the United States in the summer of 1940. Then the passage was from apathy to belligerence; today it is the reverse. This change has been fully evident only in Asia and Africa: only there has it been clear beyond a doubt that the number of nations is diminishing which are prepared to rely on the military protection of the United States. In Europe, the loss of confidence in American leadership has been muted and obscured by the prestige of the elderly statesmen who still dominate public opinion—Macmillan, Adenauer, and de Gaulle. In the United States itself, the thought of a reduction in America's standing has been so unbearable that it has been expressed only in whispers or—as in President Kennedy's case—in terms of an immediate assurance that the trend will be stopped. The full implications of a vast turning of the tide have been neither properly faced nor adequately absorbed into the national consciousness.

The launching of the Soviet earth satellite five years ago and the subsequent Russian achievements in outer space have been symbols rather than practical manifestations of a decisive alteration in the relative standing of the superpowers. Alongside the cumulative Soviet advance in industrial production, these feats have driven home the conviction that the United States no longer ranks first among the nations. Whether this is actually true can be debated. The important point is that most of the world seems to think that it is true— or that it will become true during the next decade.

Why should such a thought be intolerable to Americans? Why is it that most of them give heartfelt assent to Kennedy's oft-repeated assertion during his presidential campaign of his belief in an "America that is not first sometimes, or first when, or first if," but an "America that is first, period"? Surely this is a crude and undiscriminating fashion of expressing an aspiration to greatness. And an impractical one, too. If our education has taught us nothing else, at least it has suggested that there is no point in being first in *everything*—that to try to do so is both unrealistic and self-destructive. And on what have our schools laid more stress during the past generation than on the devastating effects of an unbridled competitive urge?

Which is all to say that there is a manifest and growing gap between what we teach our children at home and what we do abroad. Or rather, the gap lies between rhetoric and actuality in our performance overseas. Or better still, there is a discrepancy between our image of ourselves and what we really are.

We like to think of ourselves as a pioneer people. The image of America we cherish is that of a new nation, sturdy and self-reliant, brimming with optimism and confidence. When some aspect of our behavior beyond our own shores contradicts this image, it grieves us, and we try to explain it away as a temporary aberration. We seldom ask ourselves what the connection of such behavior may be with the underlying character of our society and the enormous changes that have taken place in that society over the past generation. Thus, when we gradually learned that a large proportion of American prisoners in the Korean war had shown a lack of physical and moral stamina in facing their persecutors, most Americans were merely shocked and incredulous. Few were tempted to inquire whether these young men had not been brought up in such a fashion as to make their behavior in captivity quite predictable and, by the same token, deserving of understanding rather than condemnation.

Actually, we know a good deal now about the society in which we live—far more than we did a decade ago. Beginning with the publication of David Riesman's *The Lonely Crowd* in 1950, a whole succession of works of social and economic analysis have given us a new grasp of ourselves and of the communities in which we live. John Kenneth Galbraith has spelled out the implications of material plenty; Paul Goodman has explained how difficult it is in contemporary America for young people to do an honest day's work; the sociologists—with Vance Packard as their popularizer —have described the way the old personal motives of open and ruthless economic competition have yielded to a more subtle and concealed vying with one's neighbors in terms of status symbols. From a decade of observation and analysis there has emerged a clear picture of contemporary America as a satisfied, self-indulgent, and consumer-goods-obsessed society, far gentler than it was a generation ago, far more tolerant in its relations between man and man, yet at the same time rather soft, rather slack, and notably lacking in militancy. Our new defects we have discovered to be the reverse side of our new-found virtues.[1]

Most literate Americans have absorbed and digested at least part of this recent self-knowledge. What they have not done, however, is to take the mirror that Riesman and Galbraith and the others have held up to our contemporary society and to direct it toward the field of foreign policy. In foreign affairs, we have gone on behaving as though we were still a pioneer people.

1. See Seymour Martin Lipset, "Equal or Better in America," *Columbia University Forum*, IV (Spring, 1961), 21.

We have boasted of our youthful energy and linked this with a vocation for world leadership. We have failed to apply to our conduct abroad our new understanding of the vast transformation in American national character that the past generation has witnessed.

We have indeed had an experience of American world leadership, but its period was of brief duration—a decade and a half, no more. Many people thought, of course, that we were ready for it as early as the turn of the century, when the Spanish-American War catapulted the United States into international prominence. But the American people held back: for forty years both leaders and led tarried on the threshold—with the notable exceptions of Theodore Roosevelt and of Woodrow Wilson (and the latter only during his second administration). Americans refused to assume the world responsibilities that were theirs for the taking. We sometimes forget that even Franklin D. Roosevelt was a near-isolationist in the 1930's. Not until Pearl Harbor did the United States fully commit itself to the position of first among the powers to which it had long been entitled in terms of potential strength. Hence, we can date with some accuracy the period of American hegemony—the sixteen years from 1941 to the launching of the Sputnik in 1957.

Many Americans would claim that this hegemony still obtains. Partisan Democrats might add that it was forfeited—or gravely weakened—by the supineness of the Eisenhower administration. The charge has repeatedly been made that the Republicans in power frittered away the legacy of American strength and prestige bequeathed to them by Presidents Roosevelt and Truman. But such an accusation is patently unfair. True, Eisenhower and Dulles committed all sorts of errors

and did not know how to make the most of their assets: they muffed the heaven-sent (and probably un-
repeatable) opportunity of the years immediately following the death of Stalin in 1953, when the Soviet
leaders, unsure of their tenure and still outclassed in
weapons, were ready for a compromise settlement in
Central Europe. At the same time, the assets that
Eisenhower held were fewer than those at the disposal
of his predecessors—and they were dwindling. The
Republicans in power were simply not in a position to
take the sort of actions the Democrats had earlier accomplished with comparative ease.

If one looks back on the decade and a half from
1941 to 1957 and tries to observe its salient characteristics (a survey that is only now beginning to be
possible), one finds in it a unique combination of circumstances favorable to the United States. America's
older rivals for leadership—Germany and Japan, Britain and France—were either defeated in war or permanently weakened by it. The newer challengers—the
Soviet Union and China—also weakened by the struggle, needed in the one case at least ten years, in the
other case a generation or more, to mobilize their industrial potential. In the meantime, the United States
stood alone as the one great power which was not seriously hurt—on the contrary, was strengthened—by the
Second World War. The short-run circumstances of the
postwar years reinforced this situation of American
world primacy: with Western Europe turning to the
United States for economic and military aid, and with
Asia and Africa not yet figuring in the power balance,
all lines of authority seemed to converge on Washington.

During Truman's second administration, from 1949

to 1953, Secretary of State Dean Acheson gave this American hegemony its fullest and most coherent expression. His policy of support for governments of the democratic center admirably fitted the ideological configuration in Western Europe itself: Christian Democrats held the foreign ministries of all three major Continental countries—France, Italy, and Germany—and dominated the governments of the latter two; these leaders were sincerely pro-American, and the temperamental anti-Communism that sprang from their Catholic faith corresponded to a situation in which a Soviet invasion of the West seemed a real possibility. During Stalin's last years of near-paranoia, the most alarmist estimates of Soviet intentions could be entertained in good faith by men who in other respects held moderate views on foreign policy. A shared sense of uncertainty and impending peril brought Americans and Europeans together in the closest peacetime understanding that our history has known.

If in Europe the Truman-Acheson policy showed logic and coherence, in Asia it was quite otherwise. There are those who claim that the President and his Secretary of State were moving toward a recognition of reality in China just before the outbreak of the Korean war; we were on our way to coming to terms with the Chinese Communists when the North Korean attack supervened. However that may be, the invasion of South Korea undoubtedly caught the Truman administration by surprise. If a reorientation of policy was in fact in progress, the Korean war stopped it in its tracks. The conflict over Korea froze America's Asian policy in an attitude of stubborn and unimaginative military defense. There we have remained ever since —as one after another of the right-wing national leaders on whom we relied has proved either unable or unwilling to halt the advance of Communism.

The Korean war, then, while it was the logical outgrowth of the Truman-Acheson policy, also marked the decline of that policy. At home, it stimulated the resurgence of a primitive nationalism which found its master spokesman in Senator Joseph McCarthy.[2] In Asia, it ended any possibility of negotiation with Communist China. In Europe, it undercut the foreign policy of Christian Democratic leadership and of European integration: with the new military emphasis in aid from the United States—and with the American insistence on the rearmament of Germany—both nationalist conservatism and neutralist tendencies found reason for encouragement; the rule of the democratic center came under fire from two sides. The final irony of the Korean war was that America's conduct of it eventually alarmed the very Europeans whom it had been intended to reassure. The statesmen of the West who had been delighted in June, 1950, to find that the United States stood ready to honor its pledges to a threatened ally, were appalled the following November at the possibility that the war would extend into a major struggle against Communism.

By 1953, nearly everybody was sick of Korea. Perhaps the most potent of Eisenhower's campaign assets during the previous autumn had been his pledge to bring the war to an end. In so doing, the new President received accidental help from the fact that Stalin's death came only two months after his own inauguration. Beyond that, Eisenhower's concept of foreign policy—vague though it was—conformed more closely to the sentiments of the inarticulate mass of the American

2. See Chapter 11.

people than did that of either Truman or Kennedy. Eisenhower knew that his people wanted "no more Koreas." He himself was, in the depths of his being, a man of peace. And the last of the great events that made the spring and summer of 1953 a major turning point in world history—the Soviet announcement that it had broken the American monopoly of the hydrogen bomb—underlined such convictions by inaugurating the present era of thermonuclear balance of terror.

Eisenhower and, more particularly, Dulles still tried to behave as though their country's strength and influence remained the same as during the preceding Democratic administrations. But the facts gave them the lie at every turn. The completion of Soviet reconstruction and Russia's subsequent advances in weaponry, the beginnings of industrial mobilization in China, the awakening of Africa, the economic boom in Western Europe and the new sense of independence from American direction that accompanied it—all these showed that the temporary circumstances that had endowed the United States with its postwar lead were rapidly coming to an end. Secretary Dulles concealed this situation as best he could. President Eisenhower put up less of a bluff—his undisguised weariness at being in office at all mirrored his country's reduced circumstances. By the presidential campaign of 1960, the Democrats had a potent issue ready to hand: they had a free field to charge the Republicans with negligence in maintaining the American world position— a possibility of which Kennedy availed himself to the full.

President Kennedy entered the White House full of youthful confidence and pledged to restore to his country a sense of its vocation for leadership. Once again, however, the facts betrayed him. Less than three months after he had taken office, the desperate fiasco of our intervention in Cuba brought home the reality that the President and his advisors had been so reluctant to recognize: that in the changed circumstances of the 1960's the United States was no longer able to manipulate small nations at its pleasure. By the summer of 1961, America's world situation was scarcely distinguishable from what it had been in the last months of Republican rule.

America's world leadership came too late. It came too late in a double sense. First, it happened just as the postimperial age was beginning: by the 1950's, the newly liberated and ideologically uncommitted nations were no longer willing to accept direction—however veiled—by any Western power, no matter how "anticolonial" its past history and present rhetoric; all the facile talk about the United States' succeeding to the imperial mantle of Britain had become one vast anachronism. Second, by the time the American people were ready to undertake such a mission, they were no longer suited for it. The United States had delayed too long: the generation during which the Americans had held back from world leadership was the same generation which slowly but cumulatively had disqualified them for the task. The forty years in which the United States had gradually overcome its isolationism were the very decades in which the most rapid social change in its history had sapped its militancy and its pioneer spirit. In the first decade of the century, President Theodore Roosevelt had pleaded in vain for Americans to undertake the mission that awaited them. His people failed to respond—but in terms of char-

acter and enthusiasm, they were equipped for the great
adventure. Sixty years later, when President Kennedy
—a Theodore Roosevelt reincarnate—again raised the
call, his people had been embarked on a world mission
for two decades. But the force of their effort was already receding. This was the most curious irony of
American history in the twentieth century.

Much of the foregoing may sound like the lamenta-
tions of the despairing American right. And this is in
part true. I believe that many American conservatives
have a more accurate understanding of their nation
than do the self-styled liberals who live in a world of
optimistic illusion. But the tone and spirit of my observations are quite different from those of the nationalist right. *Its* position is one of agonized resolution:
the logic of its arguments runs inexorably toward a
militarization of the country and even toward preventive war. Deep down, conservatives have little respect
for or confidence in their own people. Conscious that
their personal power—and that of their nation—is slip-
ping, they are subject to the understandable temptation
to risk everything on one last desperate military gamble.

This is the truly alarming aspect of the series of
crises—Laos, Cuba, Berlin, and the rest—that we have
experienced since President Kennedy's inauguration.
Each time, the call has gone out from Washington to
"hold the line" and concede nothing. Each time, the
administration and the press have systematically played
on the simplest and most emotionally charged of patriotic themes. They have tried to arouse our people
to militancy—but only to let them down again. For in
the end we have consented to what we earlier maintained was impossible. Our talk has proved hollow:

despite all the beating of the war drums, we have accepted still another Western "defeat."

Defeat and victory depend on how one chooses to define them. To my mind, it is not a defeat to withdraw from an exposed position where we should never have been at all. But that is not the way the people in Washington see it. They define as a defeat any relinquishment of an American or Western holding, no matter how indefensible it may be or how out of date the reasons that put us there in the first place. Yet still they swallow one "defeat" after another; the illogic is patent. Thus it is not any single crisis in itself that carries the threat of war—it is the cumulative effect of a number of them on a bewildered American public. The real danger for our country will come when our nationalist right finally wakes up to the fact that it has been "had."

My convictions are almost exactly the opposite. I believe that a mood of last-ditch resolve is one of the gravest perils we currently confront. The stance of heroic despair is dangerous for the very reason that the analysis of the American character on which it rests is not wholly unfounded. My own suggestions for meeting the current emergency run in a contrary direction. I advocate playing for time—a Fabian policy, superficially lacking in heroism, but one which has rescued many a nation and many a society since the half-legendary era when Quintus Fabius Maximus (who ranks as one of Rome's heroes) first saved the Republic by a systematic policy *of delay*.

My attitude may likewise seem to imply a neo-isolationism. Again the resemblances to an American rightist position are merely superficial. Although I advocate closing down most of our existing military bases overseas—and thereby eliminating any pretext the

Russians may find for accusing us of aggressive intentions—I think we should still stand ready to come to
the aid of our true ideological associates. Moreover, the
withdrawal into North America that I propose for my
own country parallels and derives from the similar return of nations like Britain and France to preponder-
antly European interests. This is a chapter of our recent history which sometimes slips our minds: we forget
that America's world role in the 1940's and 1950's was
intimately involved with the liquidation by the European powers of their Asian and African holdings,
that our leaders felt obliged to support this process or
to fill the vacuum left after the departure of the former
white overlords. But we should also remember that the
responsibility was only temporary: by the 1970's it will
doubtless be at an end. The new world balance will
find each major region taking charge of its own concerns.[3]

This does not mean that they will be isolated from
each other. On the contrary—economic and intellectual contacts may even increase, since there will no
longer be exploitative connotations attached to them.
In this sense, my point of view is the very opposite of
isolationism: I believe that our nation should enlarge
rather than diminish its aid programs, its cultural ex-
changes, and its support for United Nations activities.
But it should do this as between equals—and with nothing asked in return.

We need to cut out a new foreign policy to fit our
cloth. We need to recognize that the human material
our nation affords is not quite the fabric we imagine it
to be. But it is still a good cloth: it has its unsuspected

3. See Chapter 6.

virtues as well as its celebrated defects. I yield to no man in my hatred of the ugliness and idiocy and waste in American life. Yet still I *like* my people. I find in America far more to love than to condemn. While my country may stand no longer for pioneer values, it represents others that I cherish more. And I believe that we can preserve those values—tolerance, humaneness, and the rest—only by abandoning our role as the imperial leaders of the embattled West and by seeking a new model for foreign policy in the experience of Sweden or of Switzerland, or even of India.

CHAPTER 3

We Have No Quarrel . . .

WE HAVE no quarrel with Communism *as an economic system*. If our government publicly proclaimed such an attitude—if we made it perfectly clear both to the American people and to national leaders overseas that considerations of economic ideology would no longer influence United States policy; if we gave assurance to everyone that collectivism, wherever and however pursued, was quite acceptable to us—the conduct of our foreign relations would be enormously simplified. For we would have sloughed off the economic doctrinairism that is currently hobbling our exchange of goods and ideas with more than half the world; by discarding what is peripheral and dispensable in our quarrel with Communism, we should be able to focus more precisely on what we find profoundly objectionable in the Communist regimes. By narrowing the points at issue, we should have clarified them: we should be in a position to distinguish—as we cannot do now—the matters on which we are ready to negotiate and compromise from those on which we must insist at all costs.

As an economic system, Communism is a perfectly respectable way of doing things. There is no need to get upset or morally indignant about it. We are called on to do no more than to apply to it the criteria by which we judge our own economic performance—efficiency and the advancement of welfare, public and private. These goals may be in conflict (we are more and more realizing how frequently in our own country they are), but at least we agree with the Communists that they are the goals to be pursued. And we are also coming to the realization that on the grounds of *public* welfare, our performance has been far from perfect. Similarly, the leaders of the Soviet Union have become more frank about conceding that in the sector of *private* consumption their record is highly unsatisfactory. The elements of a dispassionate (and even friendly?) debate on the virtues of the two competing economic systems are already at hand.

This debate would not be a mere repetition of the century-old contention between the merits of capitalism and those of socialism. For neither of the protagonists is quite what it used to be. As the capitalism of the West has become less capitalist, so collectivist doctrines and practices have grown less socialist. The traditional socialism or social democracy of Europe has lost its self-confidence and its moral drive: its official leaders have become scarcely distinguishable from their "bourgeois" opponents.[1] Perhaps for that reason they have found few imitators in the non-European world. Beyond Europe's shores, what remains of socialism's old message is little more than a few practical precepts for collectivist action. Their tone has ceased to be evangelical—it has become managerial and businesslike. In this sense, the socialism or quasi-socialism of the newly liberated countries owes far more to Soviet or Yugoslav experience than it does to that of European social democracy. And it is for this reason that I have chosen to speak of Communism rather than socialism even

1. See Chapter 7.

when discussing only its economic aspects. In tone and emphasis, the new collectivism of the underdeveloped world bears the Moscow stamp.

All but a tiny minority of Americans are apparently convinced that our current system is the better one; a growing majority of leaders in the world outside seems to think otherwise. In the coming decades, governments and individuals will be comparing statistics and making up their minds. They can do this in a fashion that to a surprising extent is now "value free." For since twentieth-century capitalism accepted the welfare state, its proclaimed values have become not notably different from those of Communism. Both in theory believe in human equality; both aim at the elimination of want; both honor production and scoff at the idler; both define the good life in terms of peace and security. The differences between them are largely technical and procedural—or of failure to live up to their own ideals. The current *economic* argument between capitalism and Communism is not really a *moral* debate at all.

If that premise is accepted, two important corollaries flow from it. The first concerns the relation of American business to the conduct of foreign policy.

I think it would be absurd to argue, as the Marxists do, that our country's foreign policy is determined above all by the needs and desires of American capitalism. But there is *something* to the argument—as there usually is with Marxism. Most of the time, economic interests are not the decisive factor in shaping American foreign policy—but they are decisive *some* of the time, and they bend or deflect policy *nearly all* the time. Examples are not difficult to find. The influence of the oil companies on our relations with the countries of the Near East is scarcely even debated. And in all the wringing of hands over Cuba that went on after the failure of the invasion attempt in April, 1961, it was tacitly agreed by both the partisans and the critics of the landing that relations between Castro's revolutionary government and the United States would not have deteriorated so rapidly if the nationalization of American enterprises had not been involved.

Besides the familiar fact that the capitalistic organization of the American economy sets up a mighty barrier against our understanding the needs and aspirations of the underdeveloped world, the largely private character of our investments abroad also creates difficulties which would not otherwise exist. The expensive living and the personal obtuseness of so many American business representatives overseas are merely the surface manifestations of a deeper problem. The basic question concerns their relationship to the government at home. Were they mere "gentleman adventurers," as English enterpreneurs called themselves in the sixteenth- and seventeenth-century springtime of imperialism—operating independently of their country's rulers and with little expectation of support from home—then they would present no particular embarrassment to Washington. Our government could either back them up or wash its hands of them, as its wider interests dictated. As it is today, however, the average American businessman investing overseas expects both to retain his personal freedom of maneuver and to receive endorsement and protection from his government at home.

Fortunately, there is a ready solution to the problem. Our government need not go so far as to give notice to all American companies that they invest overseas only at their peril and that not a finger will be lifted in their behalf should some revolutionary regime nationalize their holdings. That, however, is the logic of the solution I am proposing. Our government should certainly put the brakes on *new private* investment abroad; it should make it clear that it will not allow itself to be deflected from its course by the piteous outcries of those who have been despoiled, that it will make representations on their behalf to foreign states only if such a policy conforms to its broader objectives. But our government need not leave American investors penniless. By a comprehensive "political insurance" measure— such as was discussed by the Congress in the spring of 1961—it can agree to underwrite companies with long-standing investments abroad that are now in peril of nationalization. It can agree to compensate its citizens for their losses—but not undertake to get their tangible property back. I have no idea what such a scheme would cost. No doubt it would be very expensive. So are most things we do in the United States. The underwriting of risky investments overseas is simply one of the prices we have to pay for clinging to our quaint business ways—and a logical extension of our contemporary economic pattern, which combines a residual devotion to free enterprise with an insistence that the good society should cushion the risks of life for all its citizens.

The second corollary concerns the character of neutralist leadership. I am far from claiming that the general caliber of the emerging leaders of revolutionary or quasi-revolutionary governments in Asia, Africa, and Latin America is inspiring from either the political or the ethical standpoint. I do not see much reason for ad-

miring Nasser or Sukarno or Nkrumah or Castro. I
quite agree with Henry Kissinger that a wave of senti-
mentality about the neutrals threatens to engulf us,
that we are wrong if we ascribe to them any particular
virtue or a special wisdom that will enable them to
solve international problems for which they have only
small intellectual and technical preparation.[2] At the
same time, I do not concur in the view of one British
publicist that these people are no more than a collec-
tion of political "mountebanks." I think rather that they
are extremely difficult men to get along with. There are
all sorts of explanations for this in their own past sufferings and the sufferings of the people they are now leading, and we shall not arrive at a balanced judgment on
them unless we try to understand how they came to be
as they are. All the understanding in the world, however, will make them only slightly less difficult. Even if
we approach them with every possible courtesy, we
are more than likely to be met with truculence.

Yet it is absolutely necessary that we do try to live
with them. There is no realistic alternative: our policy
of supporting elderly oligarchs from the landholding
class has obviously failed.[3] Neutralist leadership in the
underdeveloped world is beginning to fall into a pattern: these men are enormously confident, unscrupulous, voluble, intellectually amorphous, and largely
self-taught in the ways of collectivism. Moreover, the
pattern seems to be spreading. Truly liberal and large-
minded men are growing rarer. Americans may find it

2. See *The Necessity for Choice* (New York: Harper & Brothers, 1961), pp. 329-339.
3. One of the earliest and most lucid analyses of this situation
was provided by G. L. Arnold (George Lichtheim) in *The Pattern of World Conflict* (New York: The Dial Press, Inc., 1955),
Chapter VI.

intolerable to have Castro as a neighbor for any lengthy period, but I should wager that we shall have more Castros to reckon with before we have fewer.

Precisely here would lie the advantage of dropping our hostility to Communism as an economic system. Setting up a distinction of this sort between the tolerable and the hateful features of Communist or near-Communist regimes would enable us to make similar distinctions in our attitude toward those regimes. The very fact that we would accept with equanimity the nationalization of American enterprises would free us to express our point of view more vigorously on violations of basic human rights (which, most people now agree, do not include a right to hold large property). We would no longer be vulnerable to the old accusation of a special hypocrisy inherent in Anglo-Saxon speech. The disinterestedness of our concern for individual human beings suffering oppression would be far more apparent once it could no longer be dismissed as a smoke screen for economic egoism.

Moreover, the charting of such distinctions would give us ideological elbow room. Although the more dynamic leadership of the newly liberated or newly awakened states runs to pattern, the practices of these states cover a wide spectrum, extending all the way from doctrinaire collectivism (as in Cuba) to pilot collectivist experiments (as in Ghana) and from the exercise of naked terror to no more than sporadic arbitrariness on the part of the police. Our country needs to reckon with these complexities; it must understand all the ramifications of ideological and racial passion at work in Asia and Africa and Latin America. Only the most flexible of policies, carefully attuned to the qualitative differences that distinguish each area and political

movement from another, will enable us to steer through
eddies of mass emotion which will doubtless grow even
more treacherous during the years to come.

Finally, a recognition that Communism is a tolerable
form of economic organization would free us from the
prejudice that has made us condemn so many of the
new regimes as "undemocratic." I am quite ready to
grant that most of these regimes do not conform to any
of the customary definitions of democracy. But I cannot associate myself with the self-righteousness that usually accompanies such assertions. I think we should
ask ourselves, rather, what the alternatives are and how
practicable classical democracy may be in new nations
lacking political experience and hampered by low literacy and living standards. To ask the question is already to find the answer. We may recall that even
such shining examples as India and Tunisia—which
have had the advantage of an extensive educated class
to draw on—function essentially as single-party states
under the guidance of a benevolent leader whose wisdom remains unquestioned.

Beyond the rather elementary matter of the present
feasibility of democracy, we should also raise the
deeper issue of the future possibilities inherent in these
regimes. I suggest that a useful criterion for judging
them would be to assess their capabilities of change—
their potential for evolving into systems more conducive
to human freedom than the one-party rule that seems
to be becoming the norm. Here the crucial distinction
is not economic at all: it is, rather, intellectual and
spiritual. To take a European example, most of us entertain varying degrees of hope that Poland will one
day find its way to internal freedom. Yet Poland is a
highly collectivized state—at least in its cities. We do

not hold out such hopes for a large number of countries, governed by military cliques, whose economic practices conform more closely than those of Poland to our own. The difference is, of course, that Poland has what most of the nations run by generals do not possess—an intellectual elite whose yearning for freedom is manifest and whose influence on public policy is far from negligible.

Such an evolution toward freedom, we should recognize, may be so different from ours that we may not appreciate it properly when it comes. Parliamentary democracy—or presidential democracy of the American type—does not exhaust the possible forms that free government can assume. There are other conceivable models: the new African states are experimenting with them in an effort to take account of such local peculiarities as tribal jurisdictions and allegiances.[4] Perhaps the institution of a single charismatic leader may outlast the era of his unquestioned power. Surely the emergence of a similar type of nationalist spokesman in so many widely separated parts of the globe suggests that these figures respond to some inner necessity, especially among non-European peoples. Perhaps a suspicion of the "cult of personality" (the Soviet reference is intentional) is a very late development in the political evolution of newly liberated communities. At least we should keep our minds open. And in liberating our imaginations to speculate on the future, nothing will help us more than to leave at home those economic preconceptions that are currently confining our vision of the world beyond our shores.

*   *   *

4. See Herbert J. Spiro, "New Constitutional Forms in Africa," *World Politics*, XIII (October, 1960), 69-76.

Our real quarrel with Communism scarcely needs to be defined. It has been implicit in all the foregoing discussion. Our real quarrel is with Communism's tyranny over the mind of man. And I mean this in the widest sense. I mean terror and censorship, arbitrary imprisonment and forced labor, the falsification of history and barefaced lying in international assemblies—every aspect of conduct and policy that is inhumane and deceitful. I am quite ready to agree with the most militant of anti-Communists that in this sense Communism is indeed a "scourge" or a "poison," a dreadful affliction of contemporary humanity.

I think it most important that anyone who advances views such as mine should formally put these things on record—that he should express his unqualified condemnation of Communist brutality and perversion of the truth and that he should dissociate himself from every effort to apologize for them or explain them away. It goes without saying that the moral condemnation must be even-handed: it implies a similar outspokenness regarding the conduct of our own countrymen or that of our allies. Where Western policy has violated the elementary principles of civilized behavior among peoples—whatever the provocation—the same moral standards apply as in judging the crimes of Communism. The French and American intellectuals who condemned the war in Algeria in 1960 and the intervention in Cuba the following year showed a sure sense of where the central ethical issue lay—they were right in shattering the national consensus in their home countries. There has been no more desolating evidence of an erosion of democratic procedures over the past two decades than the spreading conviction that patriotic citizens should refrain from "rocking the boat" by exposing their own government's misdeeds and follies.

Where I differ with the militant critics of Communism is in not regarding the system as all of a piece. I have already tried to distinguish its economic practices from its terrorist features. More broadly, I believe that the various aspects of Communism are separable and that the system as a whole is capable of evolving in a liberal direction. Indeed, since the death of Stalin such an evolution has been in progress. Admittedly, it has been confined to Europe and it has several times been interrupted or reversed, but the net effect over the past decade has been a cumulative shift toward a more tolerable life. In this change lies the still dim but ever more discernible hope for humanity in the next half century. It is obviously a change that we Americans should welcome and encourage. And one way of encouraging it is to refrain from needling the Soviet Union or its representatives on their day-to-day authoritarian routines—to restrict our condemnation to the most notorious incidents, such as the repression of the Hungarian revolt in 1956, in which a wholesale violation of liberty has set back the entire process of Communist evolution toward more humane behavior.

The same reasoning suggests that a military crusade against Communism would have the very opposite of a liberalizing effect. Far from urging them to milder courses, it would stiffen the backs of the Communist rulers. Yet, if we eliminate a military solution, how are we to defend human liberty? How are we to stand for the values of the West that we can sacrifice only at the cost of losing our own souls? How are we, finally, to draw a line of no retreat? This is the deepest and most tormenting problem that the critics of our nation's foreign policy confront—and one that we must approach with utter candor if we are not to be dismissed (and rightly so) as honeyed deceivers who are lulling our countrymen to sleep.

CHAPTER 4

The Strategy of Deterrence

THE PAST two years have seen the publication of a spate of books on war, armaments, and the future course of American foreign policy. They have in common a sense of urgency—a sense that the nation has reached a major point of decision, in which the old and tried formulas no longer suffice. Certainly the turn of the decade, coinciding with a presidential election year, has helped inspire this conviction of unaccustomed challenge. In addition, there has been the mounting suspicion that the United States has slipped behind in its competition with the Soviet Union—in the arms race, in economic expansion, and in winning friends among the new or uncommitted nations—and, with it, a widespread doubt as to whether our government itself knew where it was going. Finally, the launching of a militant "peace movement," extending through a wide gamut of organizations from the sober and cautious Committee for a Sane Nuclear Policy to the more radical Committee of Correspondence, has shown the need for a counteroffensive on the part of the "cold warriors" and the proponents of a dynamic defense policy.

The current flood of new books, then, has had to take into account both confusion in public policy and the challenge from peace and disarmament spokesmen. The result has been salutary: the level of discussion

has gone up, and the great debate of the 1960's
which these books have inaugurated promises to com-
bine an unprecedented technical sophistication with a
sensitive awareness of moral ambiguities.

Some of the recent strategic studies restrict themselves to disarmament or "arms control." [1] Others survey the entire range of choices in international affairs
confronting the United States today.[2] Still others carry
the imprint of the RAND Corporation's cool and ultra-
professional assessment of risk taking: they deal with
thermonuclear war in the context of contemporary
game, decision, and communication theory, bringing
to bear on war and strategy the new logical and mathematical techniques of social science.[3] But the most important and the most troubling of the lot is that curious
book, *On Thermonuclear War,* by Herman Kahn.[4]

I think I can say without qualification that Kahn has
written one of the great works of our time. Its title
sounds like plagiary of Clausewitz' *On War,* and if Kahn
aspires to be the master military strategist of the mid-
twentieth century, I know of no better claimant. For a
number of years, as a RAND expert in the field of nuclear armament, Kahn dazzled and bewildered a series
of highly selected audiences with marathon "briefings"

1. For example, Richard J. Barnet, *Who Wants Disarmament?* (Boston: Beacon Press, 1960) and the collaborative volume, *Arms Control, Disarmament, and National Security,* edited
by Donald G. Brennan (New York: George Braziller, Inc.,
1961).

2. I am thinking particularly of Henry A. Kissinger's *The
Necessity for Choice* (New York: Harper & Brothers, 1961). It
is noteworthy that this book marks a departure from its author's
earlier insistence on the possibilities of limited nuclear war, showing a cumulative revision of his views in the direction of both
humility and humanity.

3. See Thomas C. Schelling, *The Strategy of Conflict* (Cambridge, Mass.: Harvard University Press, 1960).

4. Princeton, N.J.: Princeton University Press, 1960.

that became legendary in military circles. His book offers an almost literal transcription of three of these
lectures, plus tables, charts, priority listings, aphorisms
and asides, and explanatory appendices. From the literary standpoint, this method of presentation is far
from ideal. It entails both gaps and repetitions; the
style oscillates wildly between the overexplained and the
elliptical, the colloquial and the jargon of social and
military science, the jocular and the heavily serious.
But such has been the character of most similar great
books in the past; their message has been too over-
powering to come out in tidy form. Their very dishevel-
ment has been a mark of their significance.

What Kahn tries to do—and what, so far as I know,
no one else has tried to do in so thoroughgoing a fashion—is to look thermonuclear war in the eye and to
treat it as a reality rather than a bad dream. He asks
himself the question: after such a war, "Will the survivors envy the dead?" And he answers, no—at least if
we begin right away to take the proper precautions.
"Despite a wide-spread belief to the contrary," he argues, "objective studies indicate that even though the
amount of human tragedy would be greatly increased
in the post-war world, the increase would not preclude
normal and happy lives for the majority of survivors
and their descendants." Hence he offers us a table of
"tragic but distinguishable post-war states"—ranging
from two to 160 million dead—and he urges us to
abandon the idea that the "only choices available" are
"immediate surrender, immediate preventive war, or
eventual world annihilation." A child, he says, could
tell the difference between ten and sixty million casu-
alties, yet "few adults seem . . . able to do this." [5]

5. *On Thermonuclear War*, pp. 21, 551.

When he has pressed them, however, most Americans he has interviewed have settled on something like the latter figure as the highest they can imagine being worth a war (most Europeans set *their* total a good deal lower). And this gives him his solid starting point. Building on the notion of a "bearable" number of deaths, Kahn proceeds to analyze in rather reassuring style the genetic dangers from radioactivity and to urge the merits of a minimum program for constructing underground shelters.

Hence his book deals not only with thermonuclear war itself but with the possibilities of postwar recovery. Indeed, the most fascinating of the analytical devices he has thought up for handling his novel data concerns the "recuperative powers" of such nations as the United States and the Soviet Union. Each, he says, can be divided into "two countries, an 'A' country consisting of 50 to 100 of the largest cities, and a 'B' country made up of the remaining rural areas, towns, and small cities. . . . While the A country cannot survive without a B country, the B country can not only survive without the A country; it also seems to have the resources and skills it needs to rebuild the A country in about ten years. . . . In fact, the problem the B country faces in rebuilding the A country is probably less difficult than the one met by the Soviet Union in constructing the Soviet Union of 1955 from its 1945 base." [6] For the United States, such a job of reconstruction would be a bit harder; we are a more urbanized nation. But the difficulties would still not be insuperable.

The reader's first reaction is to be appalled by the apparent callousness of such statements. It is true that

6. *Ibid.*, pp. 77-78.

Kahn underestimates the effects of frightful devastation
on the emotions of the survivors. Despite his efforts to
convey to us the notion of thermonuclear war as a present reality, he is unconvincing in his suggestion that a
nation such as our own, after losing its great urban centers and a third of its people, would go briskly about
the task of picking up the pieces. The survivors, he tells
us, could be mobilized for effort by the reassurance of
radiation meters (which he finds even more urgent
than shelters for a civil defense program). And he cites
a hypothetical conversation with a man apparently in a
state of postattack shock: "You have received only ten
roentgens, why are you vomiting? Pull yourself together and get to work." [7]

Yet we should be wrong merely to recoil in protest.
As Kahn most persuasively argues, the notion that it is
"all too horrible" has barred the way to a proper understanding of the perils we confront.[8] On the one hand,
it has encouraged a doctrinaire pacifism. On the other
hand, and far more dangerously, it has produced among
military men and policy makers a tragic all-or-nothing
stance—the conviction that we and the Soviet Union
are linked by a "mutual suicide pact." Kahn's insistence
that there are other choices available is echoed, from
widely differing standpoints, by every qualified writer
on thermonuclear strategy. All believe that something
can be done to save us from annihilation. Yet none of
them is willing to abandon our current policy of thermonuclear deterrence. Deterrence remains at the center of all arguments: to appreciate their more specific
recommendations, we must understand first what the

7. *Ibid.*, p. 86.
8. *Ibid.*, p. 116.

experts mean by deterrence and where and when they think it should be applied.

"Deterrence," we learn, "requires a combination of power, the will to use it, and the assessment of these by the potential aggressor. . . . There can be no gap in deterrence. Deterrence is either effective or it is not. There is no margin for error. Mistakes are likely to be irremediable. If the gains of aggression appear to outweigh the penalties even once, deterrence will fail." [9]

It is likewise with the limits to the deterrent ideal. "The notion that there is only *one* form of deterrence —the threat of nuclear retaliation—must be abandoned. . . . Flexibility in both diplomacy and strategy requires that a maximum number of stages be created between surrender and Armageddon." [10] It is Kahn in particular who elaborates these stages. A large part of his book is devoted to explaining the distinctions between "minimum" and "finite" deterrence, and between a "credible first strike capability" and a largely mythical capability which relies on the mere *existence* of thermonuclear bombs. [11]

There is too much of the latter type of thinking, the strategists of deterrence agree, in American military circles today. Kahn calls it "Maginot-mindedness" and cites the aphorism attributed to one of the high brass in the Pentagon or at SAC: "If these buttons are ever pressed, they have *completely failed* in their purpose! The equipment is useful only if it is not used." [12] American strategic doctrine, they find, suffers from both

9. Kissinger, *The Necessity for Choice*, pp. 12-13.
10. *Ibid.*, pp. 56-57.
11. *On Thermonuclear War*, pp. 4, 8.
12. *Ibid.*, pp. 17, 470.

rigidity and defensiveness; it is unprepared for the kind
of ambiguous challenge—something short of a real attack on our own country or on one of our allies—
which is the form of threat we are most likely to confront in the next decade. To unleash "the deterrent"
against such an indirect challenge would be obviously
excessive. Some writers think that we should be prepared instead to bomb selective enemy targets in the
confidence that our "preattack mobilization base" will
be sufficiently strong to withstand the shock of our adversary's retaliation—our national "posture" should be
solid enough to make our counterchallenge "credible."
Others, while agreeing on the need to strengthen our
"posture" and "harden" our air and missile bases, emphasize rather the possibilities of limiting devastation
by restricting the types of weapons employed.

Quite naturally, then, these writers are impatient
both with Dulles-type threats of "massive retaliation"
and with the bland diplomacy by round-robin travel
which Eisenhower inaugurated after his Secretary of
State's death. By implication, they are scarcely less
critical of the Truman-Acheson policy of "contain-
ment." I agree that the past decade and a half has
been an almost unbroken succession of American mistakes and missed opportunities. Even granting that, the
literary strategists of 1960 and 1961 offer small comfort for the future. Nearly all the proposed substitutes
for a conventional strategy of deterrence they reject as
mere palliatives, or even as remedies more dangerous
than the disease. Disengagement, a ban on testing,
disarmament through inspection—none of these stands
the test of their disabused analysis. The net impression
they convey is bleakness itself: no obvious solution will
work; there are no short-cuts to salvation.

What is left? Only self-imposed limits on weaponry and the new shibboleth of "arms control"—a term which is fast replacing "disarmament" in the language of the *conoscenti*. It is arms control or nothing, if, as Kahn graphically puts it, we are ever to reach 1975.

Yet, when these authors begin to elaborate their specific arms control proposals, something quite different from a disarmed world emerges. The main goal, it appears, is not a reduction of weapons. It is stability and symmetry and invulnerability. The greatest danger of conflict arises, not when arms are at a peak, but when one side or another has a "weapons system" that is vulnerable to surprise attack; the very worst situation of all is a state of "mutual vulnerability." Hence it may actually be necessary at times to raise the level of armaments rather than to lower it. Specifically, in the case of missiles, we must be sure that each side has enough for a second try: "The larger the number on both sides, the greater is the absolute number of missiles expected to be left over for retaliation in the event that either side should strike first, and therefore the greater is the deterrence to an attempted first strike." [13] Similarly, with a greater number of missiles at large, the chance of one side's cheating is reduced.

Cheating, of course, is the *bête noire* of the arms controllers. It is curious that the strategists of deterrence find it possible to be such persuasive advocates of arms control at the same time as they seem to believe in the almost unlimited guile of the Soviet Union. The schemes they propose are fascinating in their elaborateness and technical sophistication; I find myself particularly attracted to a plan for "inventory" inspection, whereby each side would check at intervals

13. Schelling, *The Strategy of Conflict*, p. 236.

on the size and character of its opponent's armory, which would be collected for the purpose in specified areas. A fixed and complicated protocol would govern such transactions: "Where trust and good faith do not exist and cannot be made to by our acting as though they did, we may wish to solicit advice from the underworld, or from ancient despotisms. . . . The ancients exchanged hostages, drank wine from the same glass to demonstrate the absence of poison, met in public places to inhibit the massacre of one by the other, and even deliberately exchanged spies to facilitate transmittal of authentic information." [14]

Would safeguards drawn from classical or gangster inspiration, I wonder, ever be sufficient to foil the endless inventiveness our literary strategists attribute to the Soviet adversary? Kahn in particular seems to take a perverse delight in detailing all the dirty tricks our potential enemy might play on us—altering the weather, "spoofing and jamming" to confuse our defense system, even despatching "juvenile delinquent Eskimos" to destroy Arctic radar installations. Have the Russians *really* thought up such stratagems? Or are our military theorists perhaps suggesting to them ideas for cheating which they might never have come to on their own—as, I understand, happened when the American technical delegation wrecked a test ban agreement that was all but reached, by suddenly advancing the theory of the "big hole"? Our strategists are trying to have it both ways. They are attempting to convince us both that the Soviet Union is bound to cheat and that we can find adequate measures to cope with such cheating.

Ultimately, then, the complex reasoning of the strategists of deterrence boils down to two irreducible points.

14. *Ibid.*, p. 20.

First, there is the nightmare that perpetually hangs over us—Soviet nuclear blackmail, perhaps accompanied (as a grim token of serious intention) by the evacuation of their cities, at which, it appears, they are far more adept than we. Second, there is the distant goal of safety: in Kahn's words, "Many who have thought about this problem [and other, parenthetical references suggest he is one of them] have come to the conclusion that reliable stability can only come through an international agency with an effective monopoly of force, or total disarmament." [15] Between these two ultimates lies the vast gray area of fear and doubt in which all men of good will—whether unilateralists, multilateral disarmers, or arms controllers—now find themselves condemned to live.

It would be easy—all too easy—to dismiss the strategists of deterrence as bloodthirsty men who have computing machines where their hearts should be. *I* know that this is not so; I am personally acquainted with most of them, and I know that they are both intellectually honest and morally responsible. In terms of intellectual rigor, the only fault I find in them is a tendency to slant their interpretations in favor of the United States. In terms of moral choices, I need say no more than that they have made the opposite choice from mine. But this does not mean that I think them immoral—far from it. Faced with the frightful dilemmas of peace and war today, the best any man can do is to make his personal choice in the agony of his own conscience, convinced that whatever he does will be in some sense wrong; that, like Pascal, he is making a desperate wager in the dark, and that no one will forgive him if

15. *On Thermonuclear War*, p. 494.

he proves to have been in error.

The new strategists of deterrence offer one of the best reservoirs of brains in the country. Alongside their reasoning, the arguments of most "peace" people seem vacuous and sentimental. The advocates of peace and disarmament will never be taken seriously until they can meet and answer the authority of a Herman Kahn. I should like to make a beginning in that direction. For I believe that there are cracks in the impressive façade of deterrence apologetics—cracks which the strategists themselves are honest enough to recognize but whose implications they have not fully spelled out.

I noted a moment back Kahn's rather surprising suggestion that "reliable stability" can come only through total disarmament or a supranational authority. In the short term, then, there will be no stability. By 1973, he warns us, we shall be living in a world in which "there are quite likely to be about 50,000 ready missiles . . . , each with its own button." [16] Unless in the meantime a nearly foolproof system of arms control has been established, the "balance of terror" a decade hence promises to be more terrible than what we are living under today.

In such a situation—if I have not completely misunderstood the reasoning of Kahn and the others—the mutual annihilation or "mutual suicide pact" which they have tried to exclude as a present-day possibility would have become the dominating reality of our lives. We should be forced to ask ourselves a question that is almost taboo today: are the matters at issue between us and the Communist world worth such a sacrifice? At the present time, it appears, most Americans think so; they are prepared for the deaths of ten to sixty mil-

16. *Ibid.*, p. 514.

lion of their fellow countrymen in a slaughter which would indeed fall short of Armageddon. In another half generation, will they feel the same way about a truly apocalyptic battle?

Here a less contentious writer offers a helpful suggestion: it is Thomas E. Murray, a member for seven years of the Atomic Energy Commission, where he became known as the "conscience" of that body. A devout Catholic, Murray is gravely concerned with the moral implications of nuclear responsibilities. He reminds us of the theological distinctions between just and unjust wars, three of which are relevant here. First, will more good be accomplished by fighting than by refusing to fight? Second, will the violence applied be no more than is strictly necessary to achieve its end? Third, will "the degree of force employed . . . bear some proportionate relation to the injustice . . . perpetrated"? [17]

All of these questions, I think, have to be answered in the negative in the case of any foreseeable conflict between our country and the Soviet Union. What does this leave us, then? No more than reliance on a mutual trust which the strategists of deterrence dismiss as a snare and a delusion. Murray, like the others, has little confidence in Russian promises, but he at least thinks it worthwhile to remind us of the further theological requirement that "good faith be kept with an enemy." If good faith remains both our inescapable moral duty and the only hope we have, we need to take another look at Soviet public statements and at the current Soviet "posture," to see whether there may not be something in them that the strategists of deterrence have missed.

17. *Nuclear Policy for War and Peace* (Cleveland: The World Publishing Company, 1960), p. 29.

Kahn makes a great deal of the fact that in the past five years the Russians have been taking the possibility of nuclear warfare with deadly seriousness and "claim to have given every adult in the Soviet Union between 20 and 40 hours of instruction in civil defense." [18] In his view, this means that Khrushchev and his colleagues are prepared to use blackmail or "dirty trick" tactics and thereby run the risk of thermonuclear retaliation. But such evidence can be read differently. It can suggest a genuine fear of attack, more particularly with the spread of nuclear arms to America's European allies. Communists, unlike Nazis, have never made a cult of war for its own sake, and the economic burden of the arms race and the threat of the extension of nuclear weapons to further powers offer powerful arguments for restraint in military policy.

There is a case, then, for a minimum trust in the Soviet Union. Indeed, the strategists of deterrence seem to recognize it when they imply that a thermonuclear war would be terminated after one or two "strikes" back and forth. Peace would evidently be negotiated in the traditional fashion, and the two nations would go about the business of disposing of their millions of dead and repairing their battered economies. The picture is too "normal" to be credible. Are we really to believe that after sustaining the most dreadful physical and psychological shock of human history, the populations of the United States and the Soviet Union could settle down once more almost as though nothing had happened? What about the boundless grief and the madness and the despair? (I am reminded of the Black Death and the sense of hopelessness that settled over Europe in the mid-fourteenth century.) It is no more

18. *On Thermonuclear War*, p. 131.

difficult to give some credence to Soviet professions of faith than to believe in the vision of a postwar future conjured up by the strategists of deterrence.

The same is true with the never-never land of arms control. I find it impossible to imagine a world in which each side carefully nurtures a "weapons system" which it will never use, while its putative enemy stands watchfully by with a benevolent avuncular interest. In such circumstances, I think, life itself would begin to serve these systems: their cost, both economic and psychological, would be so enormous that rulers and peoples would eventually find the greater part of their energies absorbed in perfecting and guarding a vast establishment that served no rational purpose—or rather, one that served a purpose so exquisitely rational that somewhere along the way its original logic had been lost. By then, as David Riesman puts it, we would be in the realm of "mad rationalism."

As the theory of arms control has a specious air of logic, so it holds out a false promise of stability. Even its apologists find it adequate only in a bipolar world and wrestle in vain with the problems of spiraling technology and of an "nth" nuclear power—most obviously Germany or Communist China. Arms control is not simply another word for disarmament. It is a substitute for disarmament, and an equivocal one at that; it is an "essentially military plan, . . . a new theory for the international arms race." [19]

Rather than following the will-o'-the-wisp of equal strength and "stabilized deterrence" which arms control promises, we need to look once again at real disarmament. The American scientists at the Pugwash Confer-

19. Seymour Melman, "Arms Control: The New Defeatism," *Dissent*, VIII (Spring, 1961), 116.

ence in Moscow in the autumn of 1960 came back with
the conviction that their Soviet opposite numbers were
in earnest about disarming and that the Soviet government had made disarmament a central policy goal.
The Russian technical men, they found, worried about
the same things as the Americans—nuclear arms in the
hands of nth powers, a war brought on by accident,
the spiral of technological advance—and they were re-
ceptive to the idea of finding a compromise between
the American insistence on establishing an inspection
system *before* disarmament and the Soviet emphasis on
immediate progress in arms reduction.[20]

In this connection, a few simple statements by a re-
freshingly modest and tentative student of disarmament
are directly to the point. Deterrence, he reminds us,
has not worked. It has not prevented the expansion of
Soviet influence in the Middle East, in Southeast Asia,
and in Latin America. Moreover, all partial measures
to reduce the danger of war "share a common assumption, . . . the assumption . . . that the arms race will
go on. . . . It seems plain . . . that attempts at disarmament proposals which try to hedge against all conceivable risks will not only fail to build confidence but
will actually further inflame the atmosphere. Any agreement for meaningful disarmament requires an awareness of the risks involved, as objective an assessment
of those risks as it is given to humans to make, and,
ultimately, an act of faith." [21]

"An act of faith"—such is the only solution I can
see to the irreducible dilemma in which the strategists
of deterrence have left us, with their fear of Soviet

20. See the excerpts from the January 1961 television program "Report from Moscow: Disarmament and World Security," *Christian Science Monitor*, January 25, 1961.
21. Barnet, *Who Wants Disarmament?* pp. 126-127.

blackmail on the one hand and their implication of the necessity of world order on the other. I can find no alternative to the renunciation of thermonuclear deterrence as an instrument of national strategy. The risks in such a course are appalling. There is no final answer to the argument from blackmail and to accusations of "appeasement" and "surrender." The only remotely satisfactory reply is that these risks are preferable to the horror of thermonuclear war itself. Those of us who advocate the abandonment of deterrence must realize that we have set forth on uncharted ground and that we may find ourselves pushed step by step into a moral radicalism which few of our fellow citizens will understand and which may end in transcending more than one of the loyalties that most Americans take for granted.

CHAPTER 5

The Worst That Can Happen . . .

WE AMERICANS have been trained from childhood to look on the positive side of things; the negative, the pessimistic strike us as unhealthy emanations from the philosophic swamps of Europe. It is for this reason that as a nation we have found it so difficult to arrive at a realistic conception of contemporary foreign policy—we cannot believe that the alternatives before us are so circumscribed and the possibilities of favorable solutions so limited as a detached analysis would suggest. Hence even critics who try to be tough-minded find themselves unable to resist the compulsion to offer something positive in the way of a national program.

I hope it is clear that a note of urgency and intellectual frustration underlies the whole approach in these essays. The implication is that our country's situation is even more precarious than it appears to be and that it is time to cut our losses and to make the best bargain we can—in several parts of the world—before it is too late. With each month that passes, our bargaining power grows less and the world power balance tips more heavily in our disfavor. This is also the underlying note in the writings of such informed and judicious

commentators as George Kennan and Walter Lipp-
mann. Yet in each case the writer fails to push his pessimistic analysis to its ultimate conclusion; he finds some
escape device or silver lining to temper the austerity of
his deductions. Let us try for once to drop these psychological comforts. Let us make an experiment and speculate a while on the very worst that can happen to us.

The way to start is to wrestle with the most vexing
issue of all—the matter of unilateral disarmament.

I personally have been labeled a unilateralist in the
popular press. I am quite willing to accept the label,
providing it is properly understood. Scarcely anyone, I
think, would propose unilateral disarmament as his first
choice. Obviously, a negotiated multilateral settlement
is far preferable. What has happened to those of us
who have espoused unilateralism in one or another
form is that, after years of hoping and pleading for international agreement, we have grown discouraged
about its practicability. Disarmament has been under
active discussion for more than a decade now, and the
only progress that has been made was the *de facto*
moratorium on nuclear testing which the Soviet Union
shattered in September, 1961. In the meantime, the
French paid no attention to the moratorium and went
ahead with their own atomic bomb, while a number
(variously estimated) of other nations seemed on the
way to a similar perfecting of nuclear weapons. In brief,
despite the millions of words of good will uttered in
disarmament negotiations, the arms race has continued.
Nothing has been able to break through the barrier of
mutual distrust that separates the Communist from
the Western powers.

I believe that the only way to topple this barrier is

for one side in the dispute to make a dramatic gesture of conciliation. The sole means of overcoming distrust is for one of the parties to prove by actions rather than words that it has faith in the other. Since I am an American and not a Russian, since the minuscule influence I have can be exerted only within my own country, I suggest that the United States be the one to make the gesture. I hope that somewhere in the upper reaches of the Soviet government there is someone pleading with Khrushchev and his colleagues in tones similar to mine.

Actually we give evidence of trust in the Russians every day, although we are not fully aware of what we are doing. Our tourists depart for the Soviet Union without fear, and our merchants and statesmen are tied to their Russian counterparts by a wide-ranging series of technical agreements which they are quite sure are going to be honored. In the same way we engage in unilateral acts of disarmament without knowing it. Every time we effect an economy in our armed forces or determine on a weapon whose production entails the sacrifice of some other—every time we make military dispositions that are not "symmetrical" (as the arms controllers put it) with those of the Soviet Union —we have taken a unilateral risk. The world is very risky these days, and perhaps the only way we have been able to function in it at all is by closing our eyes a great deal of the time to what we have just done.

Some of my friends who are less unilateralist than I am prefer the phrase "unilateral initiatives" to "unilateral disarmament." I think this may be a distinction without a difference—like saying one is an agnostic instead of an atheist. But if the majority of those who feel approximately as I do would rather speak of "initiatives," I am quite ready to settle for the term. Indeed, it may have greater clarity. The trouble with the phrase "unilateral disarmament" is that it suggests an all-or-nothing stance. It seems to convey the impression that we are going to strip right down to our underwear shorts without enticing hesitations along the way. Scarcely any unilateralist would advocate this; such a position is rather that of the doctrinaire pacifists, with whom people like myself work in harmony on specific issues but with whom they differ on the wider question of the role of force in human affairs. Unilateralism as I conceive it necessarily proceeds by stages—with pauses to give our potential adversaries the opportunity to respond in kind. Actually, the first moves might entail little risk at all.[1] The main point is that *something* must be done right away to prove that we are in earnest about disarmament.

Yet the logic of the unilateralist position lies ultimately in the complete renunciation of nuclear weapons. Nor will it do to hold on to these weapons while saying we will not use them—as President Eisenhower in effect did in the last five years of his presidency, following the Geneva summit meeting of 1955. This is too ambiguous; I quite agree with one of the most penetrating critics of "nuclear pacifism" that "the proposal to withdraw from the arms race while retaining the weapons already possessed, to accept relative weakness while nevertheless remaining dangerous, manages to embrace the worst of all possible worlds." [2] In short, I believe

1. The case for unilateral initiatives has been persuasively argued by Charles E. Osgood in "Suggestions for Winning the Real War with Communism," *Conflict Resolution*, III (December, 1959), 295-325.

2. Robert W. Tucker, "Nuclear Pacifism: Some Reflections on the Community of Fear," *The New Republic*, CXLIV (February 6, 1961), 24.

that we and our allies should eventually restrict our defense to conventional weapons alone.

I well know the awful risks that such a decision would involve. Every conscientious unilateralist has spent countless hours of worry over the implications of what he recommends: he can never be sure that he is right. We face a choice of evils—a choice of risks. All we can say is that to us the risks involved in depriving our country of nuclear weapons loom less threateningly than the dangers of going on with the arms race; we agree with Sir Charles Snow that if matters continue on their present course, there is almost a mathematical certainty that some of the bombs or missiles will sooner or later go off. In this world of ghastly insecurity, we would rather take our chances on nuclear defenselessness and trust to the more primitive devices by which free men in earlier ages have safeguarded their liberty. That is what next needs to be explained.

At this point of the argument people who think as I do are usually confronted with the now classic question, "Would you rather be red than dead?" I object strongly to such a formulation: it is one chosen by our adversaries to put us in the worst possible light; it eliminates all intermediate possibilites and shades of meaning. Yet I do not agree with certain of my friends that it is a question we should not answer: I believe in answering all questions, no matter how unfair and "loaded"; any other course may be interpreted as evasion or cowardice. If our adversaries want to phrase the issue that way, I see no alternative to accepting the challenge: the only possible answer is a thunderous "Yes." Certainly I would rather be red than dead—in the sense that I choose life over senseless slaughter. But should there be a chance of a meaningful death, then I might make the other choice. That is why I do not think an affirmative answer to this crude and primitive question is the same thing as "surrender."

I have said that I am not a pacifist. At the same time, I am unimpressed by war as a method of settling disputes. I take a very poor view of nearly all the wars my country has fought to date. The vast majority, I think, were avoidable and unnecessary—just about all except the Second World War. And this last was not necessary in the sense that the United States itself was threatened. Even as a vociferous interventionist during the months before Pearl Harbor, I never believed the nationalist argument that was commonly employed to persuade the American people to edge their way into the conflict. I believed, rather, that the war needed to be waged as a disinterested crusade to rescue suffering humanity in Europe. I am quite aware that this was not the way most Americans regarded the issue at the time. I am also aware that the one war to which I am inclined to give a moral pedigree is the only war in which I myself have participated.

Yet even this nearest approach to a just war that modern humanity has experienced was not free from the ethical ambiguity which clouds the purposes of the best of men when they resort to arms. Somewhere toward the middle of the conflict we and our allies lost our moral bearings. The decisive change did not come when we dropped the atomic bomb over Hiroshima in the summer of 1945: it came more than two years earlier, with our decision to embark on the mass bombardment of German cities.[3] This decision was both a

3. See Lewis Mumford, "The Morals of Extermination," *The Atlantic Monthly*, CCIV (October, 1959), 39.

crime and an act of folly. It violated the ethical precept
that the means—the application of violence—should be
proportionate to the end to be achieved; a far smaller
aerial effort would have been adequate to break the
German war machine. There is no evidence that the
terror bombing of the Reich shortened the war by a
single day; indeed, the evidence may be just the contrary—"in reducing, as nothing else could, the consumption of nonessentials and the employment of men
in their supply, there is a distinct possibility" that such
attacks "increased Germany's output of war material
and thus her military effectiveness." [4] Our bombers succeeded in destroying their targets in the reverse order
from that intended—historical and artistic monuments
first, housing next, factories last. Of course the American people did not know this; civilian consciences at
home were lulled by the story of a fantastically accurate bombsight that made possible the precise selection
of targets from high altitudes. What was sold to the
American public as "precision bombing" in fact proved
to be ruthless and indiscriminate obliteration. I think it
is worth recalling—at a time when our military justify
the resumption of nuclear testing with the argument
that they want to develop "clean" weapons—that two
decades ago they misled us about the humanitarian
character of their bombing program.

Since 1943 at the very latest, war has no longer been
war in the old sense—it has been mass annihilation. I
think we need a new name for it, as we need to take
another look at such old-fashioned words as "defense,"
"national security," and "balance of power," which

4. John Kenneth Galbraith, *The Affluent Society* (Boston:
Houghton Mifflin Company, 1958), p. 163. It is relevant that
the author was one of the directors of the United States Strategic Bombing Survey at the end of the war.

have also altered their meanings beyond recognition.[5] Weapons of mass destruction have brought about more than a quantitative change in warfare; they have transformed its *quality* almost totally. They have made obsolete the old moral language in which free men used to assert their willingness to die for their ideals.

When Patrick Henry said, "Give me liberty or give me death," he meant it quite literally. He meant that by sacrificing his life he might help set his people free; he could not have imagined a situation in which he (and tens of millions of others) would give up their lives, and liberty would still not be the result. Moreover, he meant that he and a few thousands of like-minded citizens were making a personal choice: the rest could stay on the sidelines if they so desired—as, in fact, during the Revolution, most Americans did. Patrick Henry and his friends were committing only themselves and those who felt as they did; they were not consigning to destruction, mutilation, or genetic degeneration uncounted millions among the neutrals, the unborn, and the animal world. They were not a small minority deciding the fate of vast assemblages of living beings who could never be consulted and could do no more than passively await their end. The proponents of the American Revolution were free men in a double sense—they were free to choose a freedom that was a real alternative.

Today none of this exists. Today a handful of men are indeed free to choose, in that they hold the power of decision over whether or not to push the fatal button. But they have only a vague idea of what will be the consequences of their act—even though they must

5. See Jerome Frank, "The Great Antagonism" (Pamphlet published by Promoting Enduring Peace), p. 7.

be aware that these will extend far, far beyond anything they can possibly intend or imagine. War in this new sense has grown beyond the proportions of humanity. The problem for those of us who do not renounce force entirely is to return it to a human scale.

Does this mean "surrender"? Does it mean "to invite the conquest of the world" or to offer ourselves "on a platter" to our putative enemies? (I am quoting some of the phrases that have been thrown at me in debate.) I do not think so. I do not believe that a unilateral American renunciation of thermonuclear deterrence would make nearly so much of a difference as most of my countrymen suppose. It has yet to be proved that our "deterrent" has deterred anybody from anything. I do not think it has been the threat of thermonuclear retaliation that has kept the Soviet Union out of Western Europe. What has given the Russians second thoughts about occupying West Germany or France has been the conviction that they would find themselves most unwelcome there.

The point, then, is to make military occupation too expensive a matter—both physically and morally—to be worthwhile for the attacker. The prime need is to develop a pattern of defense by conventional weapons alone that would be "credible" (to use another arms control phrase) both to ourselves and to our potential enemies. George Kennan has delineated in imaginative fashion the character of such a defense. Although he has written simply of the Western European Continent, I think his principle can be extended to the West as a whole, including our own country. If the Continental nations were left to their own devices, he surmises, the problem of their defense would be primarily one of the internal health and discipline of the respective national societies, and of the manner in which they were organized to prevent the conquest and subjugation of their national life by unscrupulous and foreign-inspired minorities in their midst. What they need is a strategic doctrine addressed to this reality. Under such a doctrine, armed forces would indeed be needed; but I would suggest that as a general rule these forces might better be paramilitary ones, of a territorial-militia type, somewhat on the Swiss example, rather than regular military units on the World War II pattern. . . . The training of such forces ought to be such as to prepare them not only to offer whatever overt resistance might be possible to a foreign invader but also to constitute the core of a civil resistance movement on any territory that might be overrun by the enemy; and every forethought should be exercised to facilitate their assumption and execution of this role in the case of necessity.[6]

It would be an understatement to say that such a proposal represents a radical departure from current American military thinking. (Moreover, I should not want to make Ambassador Kennan responsible for an enormous extension of a suggestion he advanced rather tentatively more than four years ago in quite a different context; he may well disagree completely with what I am now putting forward.) My proposal would involve a drastic reduction of our country's present overseas

6. *Russia, the Atom, and the West* (New York: Harper & Brothers, 1958), p. 63.

commitments. It would mean the liquidation of a number of our alliances. For it implies that we would come to the defense of *those nations alone which had sufficient social and political solidity* to organize and support a territorial-militia or guerrilla-resistance type of defense—that is, those nations which, without necessarily conforming to *our* definition of democracy, were based on a bond of trust between government and people strong enough to hold out against trials and temptations of unprecedented magnitude.

Such "solid" nations include the whole of Western Europe (except Spain and Portugal), West Germany, Austria, Yugoslavia, Turkey, Israel, the Commonwealth (including societies as markedly different as those of India and Australia), the Philippines, and several states of Latin America—most obviously Mexico, Brazil, and Uruguay. The list could doubtless be enlarged. Indeed, I suggest that the establishment of such a list might be a proper occupation for our Department of State the next time it is seized by one of its recurrent moods of "agonizing reappraisal."

If this "modest proposal" has far-reaching implications for our present alliance system, it has still wider consequences for our society at home. I am under no illusions as to the radical—indeed, utopian—character of my suggestions. They involve a wholesale rethinking of nearly all the assumptions, stated or tacit, of our current policy. In terms of the "sacrifices" that our leaders so often and so hollowly call on us to make, what I am proposing demands far more individual dedication than a mere raising of taxes or contraction of consumer goods—for it implies that every able-bodied American will have to equip himself to serve as a citizen-soldier in the old-fashioned sense of the term. It means something much more strenuous than the rather perfunctory part-time military training that only a small minority of young Americans are currently receiving. It entails a tangible and personal commitment to an ideal—not just passive assent to an abstract call to greatness. It means that every American will be obliged to consider war as something close at hand, rather than as an indistinct menace whose very magnitude and remoteness make for escapism or fatalistic acceptance or moral callousness; he will need to decide when and how and for what concrete and visible loyalties he is willing to lay down his life.

That is what I mean by returning war to a human scale. The militia or guerrilla type of defense I am proposing would close the gap between rhetoric and actuality in our national behavior. It would constitute a policy that both our allies and our potential enemies could understand and act on. It would tap the resourcefulness and the talent for improvised local action that have been so marked a feature of our national tradition—and that have survived, if only in scattered communities, the enormous changes in our society over the past generation. It would restore the honored practice of resistance to oppression on the part of voluntary collectivities and spontaneous self-sustaining groups. This tradition in earlier centuries ranked as the chief support of Western liberty; the Second World War revived it in militant form on the European Continent; today in our own South young Negroes have learned what a potent weapon it is in the hands of men and women who have a clear vision toward which they are struggling.[7]

7. See Michael Walzer, "The Idea of Resistance," *Dissent*, VII (Autumn, 1960), 369-373.

If the colonial wars of liberation over the past decade and a half have taught us nothing else, they have
at least demonstrated that in the contemporary world
a superiority in arms does not necessarily mean final
victory. First in Indochina, then in Algeria, small
bodies of men, poorly armed but familiar with the
countryside and supported by the local population,
have tied up for years the regular army of a major
power. The native people have known what they were
fighting for; the Europeans have been disoriented, far
from home, and uncertain of their cause. The relevance of this example for a Western democracy facing
Communist "conquest" should be apparent to all. It is
a lesson that we Americans need to ponder.

But where does this leave us in the cold war? Is it
really possible to choose to oppose the Russians with
one type of action and to refrain from doing so with
another? Aren't we engaged in a struggle for national
and cultural survival, in which such distinctions may
dangerously weaken our resolve?

I confess that I find questions like these hard to answer. I am puzzled as to how to estimate the Soviet
Union's present aims. I agree wholly neither with those
who argue that it is no longer an expansionist power
nor with the more prevalent view that the Communist
rulers of Russia have always and forever aspired to
world domination.

I think it undeniable that the Soviet Union is currently doing better than we are in the cold war. In the
major crises of the past year—Laos, Cuba, Berlin—
the Russians have scored more points than we have.
In this sense, I agree with those in our own country

who are currently sounding the alarm. I differ with them, however, in taking a less national and power-political view of the matter. The point, I believe, is not to preserve America's position as first among the powers; it is to save the free and humane values of the West as a whole. In this second respect, the situation may be somewhat less dangerous. I am quite ready to grant that Khrushchev and his colleagues would like to humiliate and down-grade the United States as a great power. I am less convinced that they intend to "enslave" us and our ideological associates in Europe and the Commonwealth. Indeed, there is a good deal of evidence that can be read in quite a contrary fashion.

When Khrushchev visited the United States in the autumn of 1959, his words of friendship carried a hidden meaning—an unspoken plea for help. He seemed to be saying, in phrases whose ambiguity was unavoidable, that in his Chinese ally he had too big a problem for him to deal with alone. Or, to put it in broader terms, he was suggesting a Soviet-American agreement for joint action to deny nuclear weapons to further powers. Obviously he could not proclaim this in public: he could scarcely even whisper it in the most private gatherings. But to ears attuned to the nuances of international speech, Khrushchev's invitation to a dramatic shift in the world ideological alignment seemed unmistakable. For a few weeks, there hovered in the air the incredible possibility of a Soviet-American understanding to enforce the peace. As the year 1960 opened, it appeared to a French observer that our country was "torn between two alliances, one official" —NATO—"the other secret and unwritten—that is, the alliance between the U.S. and the Soviet Union against war." [8]

All this now sounds like remote history. The U-2 incident the following spring foreclosed the possibility of Soviet-American understanding. In the meantime, de Gaulle had successfully exploded an atomic bomb in the Sahara desert; Eisenhower had made no more than half-hearted gestures to dissuade him, thereby quite naturally arousing Russian suspicions. Once more it was the same weary tale of missed opportunities—as in the period 1953-1955, immediately following the death of Stalin, when the Soviet leaders were unsure of their course and ready for negotiation and compromise. This second time, if we had done something serious to restrain our French allies from becoming a nuclear power, perhaps the Russians would have responded in kind by trying to hold back the Chinese. As it was, with France having joined "the club," Communist China had an unanswerable argument for doing the same: after all, when a nation that was only in the second rank of world powers had forced its way into the select circle, could the most numerous people on earth be condemned indefinitely to military inferiority?

The summer of 1960 saw the first major ideological dispute between the Communist Chinese and their Russian allies, with the latter pleading for "coexistence" and peaceful competition with the West, while the Chinese took a more militant and doctrinaire line on the question of warfare with the capitalist powers. The final communiqué summarizing the protracted discussions in Moscow seemed to mark a victory for the Soviet view. But the following months suggested a more

8. Raymond Aron, "The End of U.S. Leadership," *The New Leader*, XLIII (January 25, 1960), 14.

frightening interpretation: in return for Chinese agreement with the Russian ideological formulation, the Soviet leaders had given their assent to China's becoming
a nuclear power—hence the Russian intransigence in
the test ban negotiations with the United States in the
spring of 1961.

So we are left with the vast unsolved problem of
China—"we" meaning our country, the Soviet Union,
and mankind in general. This is the most profound of
our anxieties; alongside it our differences with the Russians seem small indeed. China today presents the great
intractable stumbling block to world settlement: by
far the largest single mass of humanity, it threatens to
dominate, to isolate from the main stream of international contact and exchange, the whole of East and Inner Asia.

A cereal diet, cloth shoes, cotton-padded clothing,
crowded quarters, a mass life are in store for the
Chinese people as far ahead as one can see. The
private automobile age, just dawning in Russia,
will never reach China. It will remain a Spartan,
embattled have-not country, in which great public works, imposing monuments and "socialist"
achievements will have to substitute for personal
material comforts. . . .

In turn this economic difference in consumption
levels will tend to widen the great cultural gap between Chinese and Western or world civilization.
As one travels through South and Southeast Asia
one finds that the main cultural frontier lies not between Europe and Asia but between the rest of the
world and the Chinese culture area, East Asia.
. . . South and Southeast Asian nations have had

a direct contact with European countries which
has left their legal systems, their urban intellectual
life, their modern art and literature . . . in the
same world with European culture. . . . All in all,
partly because of its sheer size, partly because of its
long-continued tradition, partly because of its self-
sufficient variety and richness of culture, Chinese
civilization even in communist garb bids fair to
remain the one world area most distinctive from
all other areas.[9]

We in this country have scarcely begun to confront
the meaning of Communist China for the contemporary world. Perhaps even the Russians are just taking
their first steps in that direction. (From our own national experience, we are familiar with the device of
thinking in closed compartments, when to put such
thoughts together brings intolerable pain.) We do not
know whether the Soviet leaders fully realize as yet
what they are up against. Do they quite appreciate
China's military and economic potential and the rapid-
ity of its technical advance? Here their own recent
history should serve as a guide and a warning. Just as
the tempo of Russian progress in industry and weapons
surpassed the expectations of most Western observers,
so the Chinese may in turn surprise their Soviet allies.

What Russia did to America after 1957, China may
do to the Soviet Union in a very short span of years—
that is, challenge a newly-won hegemony which seemed
more secure than it actually was. For ordinary Russians
the prospect must be heart-breaking: just when the

9. John K. Fairbank, "Communist China and Taiwan in
United States Foreign Policy" (Brien McMahon Lecture, University of Connecticut, November 21, 1960), 20-21.

pressure on them is at last lifting—when after nearly half a century of sufferings and deprivations, a chance for personal security and a better life at last looms on the horizon—to begin once again the familiar round of economic and psychological mobilization against a threat from abroad. In a different way, the thought should be equally sobering to Americans. For it suggests that we need to rethink our stereotypes about the Soviet Union, more particularly our conception of it as a revolutionary power bent on "infinite expansion."

Here the growing ideological rift between Russia and China is of crucial importance. It means that Soviet Communism is being outflanked on the left—that it is being pushed toward the "center" of the international political alignment. I think it probable that in the next few years most of the world's Communist parties will repeat this cleavage: in nearly every country there will emerge a "hard," revolutionary faction loyal to Peiping as opposed to the "moderates" who will look to Moscow for guidance. The monolithic character of international Communism is already breaking down: in the coming decade it will doubtless disintegrate still further.

The dispute with the Chinese has both reflected and intensified the Russian people's evolution toward attitudes similar to our own. Soviet society is becoming more humane and more satisfied; the long-promised consumers' paradise is taking on reality at last. And with the first tokens of affluence the Russians are acquiring a stake in the established order—more particularly in the preservation of peace. Similarly in its international actions, the Soviet Union is beginning to behave like a "have" power. Even when it sounds

most threatening—as over Berlin—its real purpose
may be more conservative than appears on the surface.
In precipitating the Berlin crisis, I believe, Khrushchev
was not intending to upset the international equilib-
rium; he was aiming to freeze the *status quo* of a
divided Germany and a divided Europe.

If only we can preserve the peace for a few more
years, the United States and the Soviet Union may come
to recognize the interests and aspirations they have in
common. I have heard that at Moscow University the
American students find a warmer welcome than the
Chinese. I am not surprised. For in contrast to the
desperation and ruthlessness of Communism in China,
its Soviet counterpart is evolving toward values that
resemble ours. Faced with the new threat on their left,
the Russians are edging their way to a Communist
"liberalism" which may finally transform co-existence
from a propaganda slogan into a living reality.

I do not want to be misunderstood. The Soviet-
American alignment I have in mind would not be
primarily military in character: it would not try to
"contain" the Chinese by coordinated threats of nuclear attack. To do so would be to violate every principle which these essays have been urging. I mean,
rather, that the Russians and ourselves should cooper-
ate in the "domestication" of China—in raising its
standard of living, for example, through an international program of economic aid. One might even imagine something as extraordinary and paradoxical as a
joint sponsorship of Communist China's admission to
the United Nations. For until the Chinese are physically
and morally present in the chief forum of East-West
conciliation, the process of their adaptation to a new
world order cannot even begin.

*   *   *

The proposal I have made for the non-nuclear defense of our own country and our allies will, I hope, never have to be applied. I think of it as a final deterrent to aggression—a real deterrent, as opposed to the abstract deterrent of our hydrogen bombs, which is too gruesome to be fully credible. There is a simpler road to national and international survival—a Soviet-American understanding for the preservation of the peace. This offers the most realistic, indeed the only hope of forestalling the very worst that our future may hold.

CHAPTER 6

A Look into the Future

IN CONCLUDING this reconnaissance into the ultimate reaches of our anxieties, I should like to speculate for a few moments on what the world will look like a generation from now. It may be that the developments I anticipate will manifest themselves earlier than that. There is apparent in our time an acceleration in human events which Henry Adams first noticed more than half a century ago and which since then has been steadily gathering momentum. That is one reason why a number of the recent predictions of qualified observers have hit so wide of the mark. The substance of their forecasts has been accurate enough; their timetable, rather, has been at fault. Thus the advance of Communism into the newly liberated colonial world, the spread of thermonuclear weapons to further powers, the launching of human beings into space—all these have been anticipated with greater or lesser accuracy. What has surprised and disconcerted people—more particularly, us Americans—has been the speed with which such changes have come about.

No one can make predictions without assuming that the raw material of his forecasts still exists. In everything I say I shall presuppose the continuity of civilized society. It may well be that this assumption is quite false. It is more than possible that the scourge of ther-

monuclear war will descend on us and obliterate a
great part of our cities and the fabric of our society.
If that happens, all predictions will prove catastro-
phically in error. We shall wonder how we could possibly have said the silly things we did or put on paper
such grossly optimistic reflections—that is, if some
scraps of the paper on which they were printed have
survived the flames. We have yet to form in our minds
a convincing picture of a nation or a world in the back-
wash of a thermonuclear attack. Even the courageous
Herman Kahn—who has tried to make us face thermonuclear warfare as actuality rather than nightmare—
has offered too fragmentary and too reassuring an
estimate of its consequences. One of the most urgent
intellectual tasks that confronts us today is to compare
the "hard" assessments of the new intelligentsia of
self-constituted experts on thermonuclear warfare with
the apocalyptic warnings of the equally self-appointed
spokesmen for peace, and to try to find some common
ground of solid prediction. Such an effort extends
beyond the scope of the present essays. I merely suggest
that the job needs to be done.

Both the military strategists and the peace people
agree that without a world authority competent to enforce a stringent multilateral system of disarmament
there will be no surcease of fear in our time. Rather,
the danger of war will mount with each year that
goes by. The analysts of thermonuclear war vest their
hope in complex devices based on mutual distrust,
which they prefer to call "arms control." The spokesmen of the peace organizations argue for trust in our
putative enemies as the less dangerous in a choice of
evils. Both analyses, however, are almost equally desperate: neither the war planners nor the strategists of

peace see much hope that their advice will be followed. For the short run, they are skeptical and discouraged; for the far future, they are utopian. The middle time span remains uncovered.

I agree that multilateral disarmament and world government are the imperatives of the hour. I also agree that they are unlikely to be attained. Beyond that I have a visceral conviction that the big bang will not go off—that some final residue of reason or humanity will stay the hands of those in power from pressing the irrevocable button. Or perhaps they will try it just once. After one great city has been destroyed on each side—after the superpowers have traded blows and experienced as reality what before was only strategic calculation—they will sicken of what they have done and conclude that *anything* is better than fighting another such round. Sometimes I am almost tempted to wish that so ghastly a thing will happen. Humanity may not come to its senses until the unutterable has actually occurred.

Let us presuppose, then, that our physical and social world still exists a generation from now. What will it look like? I think it will differ in two important respects from the world we know today. It will no longer be a bipolar world, and within it the concept of the nation-state will have changed profoundly. These are things we mostly take for granted when we discuss international politics. We assume that the hostility between our country and its allies on the one side and the Communist bloc on the other will continue undiminished, and that this hostility will exhaust the sum of significant international doings. We also assume that a hundred-odd sovereign states, loosely associated in the

United Nations, form the natural constituent units of human society. Or, if we think beyond them, we jump immediately to a world authority, skipping all stages in between. I believe that there *is* an intermediate stage, and that this stage will play a crucial part in the coming decades in overcoming and transforming the present polarization of international life.

Anyone who anticipates, as I do, that we are likely to have more Communist or near-Communist states in the world before we have fewer, is obliged to explain why he finds this conclusion neither so defeatist nor so depressing as it is commonly supposed to be. The comparative equanimity with which I regard such a prospect is based on the conviction that the free world —that is, those parts of it that are truly free rather than just called such as a courtesy title because they happen to be allied with the United States—*can* be defended, and without resort to nuclear weapons; there is a point on every continent where Communist expansion will finally come up against the determined resistance of men whose devotion to freedom is more than verbal.

Beyond that, in the very process of its expansion, the Communist world itself will undergo vast changes: the process of internal liberalization that is already apparent in the Soviet Union will extend to other countries, and the divergence between Russia and China that has been in evidence since the great intra-Communist debates of the summer of 1960 will widen. Already there are three different models for imitation within the Communist world: the Russian, the Chinese, and the Yugoslav—and some might add the Polish as a fourth. As over the years various leaders of newly liberated nations turn to Communism for inspiration and ex-

ample, their eclectic borrowings will further twist or
water down the notion of party orthodoxy. A generation from now, the Communist world will no longer be
the tight ideological alliance that most Westerners still
believe it to be. It will look much more like a loose
league, or even a series of leagues, with Moscow and
Peiping functioning rather as regional centers of influence than as dictators of world policy. "Universal
world dominion," George Kennan reminds us, "is a
technical impossibility, and . . . the effectiveness of
the power radiated from any one national center de-
creases in proportion to the distance involved, and to
the degree of cultural disparity." [1]

Indeed, the world today is already more than bipolar.
A decade ago, it was roughly true that Washington and
Moscow were the sole points of authority and that the
United States and the Soviet Union held the ultimate
power of decision nearly everywhere; in the 1960's,
competing centers of influence are springing up on all
sides. I have already spoken of China. Western Europe
has similarly become more tightly knit and more independent from direction by one of the superpowers
than it was a decade ago. Japan's alignment with the
United States has also weakened. In southern Asia, and
throughout the underdeveloped world, India has
achieved a moral authority that bears little relation to
the feebleness of its armed forces. In the near East,
Nasser's Egypt has tried to extend its influence both to
the Arab world and to the newly liberated areas of
Africa south of the Sahara. And a parallel development is going on in Black Africa itself. Here two
groupings among the new nations are already in evi-

1. *Russia and the West under Lenin and Stalin* (Boston:
Little, Brown & Company, 1961), p. 276.

dence. One is moderate and Western-oriented and finds its natural leader in Nigeria, the most populous state on the continent. The other leans toward Nasser and toward Communist alliances and has its center of gravity in the trio Ghana-Guinea-Mali. Finally, in the Western Hemisphere itself, the United States for the first time in its history has discovered a serious rival: during Quadros' stormy tenure of power in Brazil, the second country of the Hemisphere—in size, in resources, in population—declared its independence of North American leadership.

I have named eight new centers of influence that are currently escaping or have escaped from the supervision of Moscow or of Washington. Another observer of the same developments might enlarge or contract the list. But I think the change I have been tracing is undeniable. The two superpowers of the period 1945-1950 can no longer call the tune. The bipolar world is fast disappearing.[2]

Moreover—and this is the second great change that needs to be observed—the emergence of regional centers of influence is profoundly altering the character of the nation-state itself. This, we may remember, was historically a *European* concept. The notion of a medium-sized area and people, bound together by common loyalties and traditions and usually by a common language, as the natural unit of political life, grew up in Europe in the period from the sixteenth to the nineteenth centuries and has only comparatively recently been extended to the rest of the world. Here it has fitted but lamely. Indeed, the two superpowers themselves—both semi-European in origin—betray through

2. W. W. Rostow makes a similar argument in *The Stages of Economic Growth* (Cambridge: Cambridge University Press, 1960), pp. 126-128.

their names based on an abstraction rather than on a language (and with the word "union" figuring prominently in both) their regional and supranational character. Elsewhere nations in the European sense have simply not existed. Beyond Europe's shores, vast multi-lingual empires have alternated with tribalism as the norm; Japan alone—perhaps owing to its island situation—rather early succeeded in converting itself into a reasonable facsimile of a nation-state.

In the non-European world, the natural and viable units were regional rather than in any true sense national—subcontinents or semicontinents linked together by the memory of a great empire or a common religion. Such were China, India, Indonesia, the Arab Near East—one might add Brazil. Yet in the post-1945 compulsion to liberate the peoples of Asia and Africa, the nation-state seemed to be the only formula available for institutionalizing the change. Thus, alongside the great natural regions or empires whose claim to independence was undeniable, other smaller areas were given parity with them as sovereign states which were in no position to enforce their theoretical freedom from outside supervision. Such were countries like Korea or Laos that had traditionally existed as satellites of a neighboring empire. Or—in quite a different category—there emerged a series of synthetic states in West and Equatorial Africa. Here national boundaries were completely artificial, cutting across tribal allegiances and corresponding to nothing more than lines of European conquest in the late nineteenth century.

The "Balkanization" of this area into nearly twenty sovereign states has been one of the great (and largely unremarked) tragedies of the past decade. In the general jubilation over the liberation of Black Africa, few people have stopped to notice the illogicality of the pattern of new nations that has resulted. Obviously, a great reshuffling of African allegiances is urgently required. Equally obviously, it has already begun. But the basis of readjustment is still unclear. Will it be along the cleavage of "Western" or "Eastern" ideological orientation that I mentioned a moment ago? Will the new states group themselves according to the languages —French or English—spoken by their ruling elites? Or will the criterion of integration perhaps be economic and geographical? Or finally—and least satisfactorily— will the groupings continue to be dictated, as they mostly are today, by the interests and ambitions of the narrow cliques of politicians currently in control?

All we can say with certainty is that the present crazy patchwork in West Africa cannot continue to exist. More broadly, the notion of an entire world organized into sovereign states, and these in turn granted membership in the United Nations, can scarcely survive the pressure of reality. The principle of one nation's being equivalent to one vote in the General Assembly offers too great a temptation to multiplying such units indefinitely—particularly since the developments of the last decade have made the Assembly rather than the Security Council the main forum for international debate and action. Some way must be found to institutionalize the role of the new regional centers of influence— perhaps through increasing the number of permanent members of the Security Council, perhaps through allotting to the larger nations additional votes in the General Assembly itself.

In any case, the emergence of ten or more major regional influences will give a new meaning to the

concept of a satellite state. Currently, and more particularly in Eastern Europe, this means a nation completely dominated by a superpower and with its own
interests sacrificed to that power's necessities in the cold
war. With the end of a bipolar world, the idea of
"satellitehood" will change drastically. For one thing,
the notion itself will gain a new respectability. The
existence of satellites in some form or other will be
implicit in the very concept of regional centers, and
since others will be doing it, the supervision of the
Soviet Union over its own satellites will begin to seem
less of an abuse. Moreover, that control may grow
milder as alternative centers of power and alternative
systems of regional leadership develop. In Western
Europe, for example, there may be no true satellites:
the theoretical equality among allies will come close to
reality—although the three greatest among them—
Britain, France, and Germany—will doubtless continue
to take the lead. Such an example so close at hand
may have an effect farther east: if Western Europe is
organized on its own basis and truly independent of
American supervision, the Soviet Union may feel justified in relaxing its grip on the belt of satellites that
currently constitute its buffer against the West.

I am well aware that at some future date the
organization of Western Europe into a regional power
bloc and the establishment of a zone of military disengagement in the center of the Continent may prove
to be incompatible goals. Both presuppose the end of
NATO in its present form: both similarly entail a
reduction of direct Amerian influence. But the first implies a Germany permanently divided, with its western
part committed to the Six-Nation community, while the

second suggests a federation of the two German states to serve as a neutral bridge between East and West. The former alternative is more reassuring from the standpoint of conventional military defense—the latter gives the satellites greater hope for their gradual release from Soviet control. In neither case is the choice one that we Americans can make. The choice lies with the German people.

In the future world I have been trying to delineate, the United States will cut a more modest figure than it does today. It will undergo (on a smaller scale) the sort of readjustment to the rise of new powers that Britain and France have already experienced. In a world grouped around ten or more regional centers—two or three of them Communist, two or three of them Western democratic, the rest somewhere in between—our country will rank as a major center, no more, no less. It will not be an unbecoming role. On the contrary, it will be a role more congenial to our national temperament and institutions than the task as embattled leader of the "free world" that we have felt obliged, with mounting difficulties, to assume during the past two decades.

In such a world the term "neutralism" will have lost its meaning. Or rather, all will have become major participants, all will have become neutrals, in the play of international events, providing how one chooses to define the term. Sometimes I have toyed with the idea that the simplest way to end the cold war would be for the United States to take the paradoxical step of unilaterally declaring itself first among the neutrals. In reality we do not need to go that far. The events of the next generation will doubtless do it for us.

This new world seems strange and threatening to us now. When we are in it, I think we shall find it a better world than the one we live in today.

II

IDEOLOGIES
OF THE
MID-CENTURY

CHAPTER 7

The Socialist Dilemma

FOR A FULL decade now—for a span of years that is gradually coming into focus as a historical epoch in its own right—the major countries of Western Europe have been living under conservative rule. This situation has created new and unanticipated problems in the functioning of democratic institutions. More particularly, it has raised an agonizing dilemma for the chief forces of loyal, constitutional opposition—the Social Democratic parties.

The turn toward conservatism came first in Italy. By his crushing electoral victory over the Communist-Socialist bloc in April, 1948, Prime Minister Alcide De Gasperi inaugurated a period of Christian Democratic rule that has persisted ever since. A year and a half later, the new state of West Germany was launched under similar auspices; here also government by Christian Democrats has proved unshakable. In June, 1951, the French electorate for the first time since the war sent a conservative majority to the National Assembly. The following autumn, the British did the same. In the British case, the reversal proved decisive: the narrow Conservative majority of 1951 was steadily enlarged in succeeding elections. In France, the trend to the right appeared to be temporarily checked by fifteen months of Socialist rule in 1956 and 1957. But this government

in fact existed on conservative sufferance, and on the
crucial issues of colonial policy—Suez and Algeria—it
followed a nationalist and imperial course. The coming
to power of de Gaulle in 1958 reaffirmed a drift toward
conservative solutions that had already been apparent
for seven years.

The result of this succession of conservative triumphs has been a "one and a half" party system. On
the surface, it tends toward the two-party norm which
Anglo-Saxons have traditionally considered ideal. And
in all fairness, one must grant that it marks a simplification of the multiparty competition which vexed
European democracy in the interwar period and was at
least partially responsible for the turn to fascist solutions in the 1930's. But the real point about the
evolution of the 1950's and 1960's has not been its
gradual elimination of minor parties as serious contenders. It has, rather, been the creation of a two-party
system with a crucial difference—a hybrid state of
affairs in which one of the parties seems to stand almost
no chance of electoral victory.

The outlines of this paradoxical situation first appeared in Germany.[1] As Chancellor Adenauer's Christian Democrats raised their electoral margin every four
years—as the Social Democrats lost in 1949, 1953,
and 1957 (and were to lose once again in 1961)—
it began to appear that the steady squeezing out of
lesser contenders was not having the expected effect
of equalizing the two major parties. The reduction of
the Communists and the Refugees, the German party
and even the Free Democrats, as important electoral
formations, simply strengthened Adenauer's existing

1. See Otto Kirchheimer, "Notes on the Political Scene in
Western Germany," World Politics, VI (April, 1954), 317-318.

lead.[2] Two years later, a similar tendency became evident in Britain. By 1959, after three successive electoral defeats—and four elections in which the Labour party had lost seats—Labour's parliamentary leader, Hugh Gaitskell, began to lament that something "almost unprecedented in British political history" seemed to be occurring.

In France and Italy, the electoral evolution of the 1950's did not follow so neat a pattern. For one thing, the existence of strong Communist parties, which remained quarantined from participation in government while still commanding more than one fifth the popular vote, kept a large segment of the electorate from effective political influence. In Italy, this situation of "frozen" leftist votes was reinforced by the fellow-traveling attitude of the main body of the Socialists. From 1948 to 1956, Italy languished in a condition approaching one-party rule, in which no effective opposition was possible. It was not until the Soviet suppression of the Hungarian revolution shocked the Italian Socialists out of their alliance with Communism that Italian politics began to approach the "one and a half party" norm. Since then, with each succeeding Socialist party congress, the evidence has been mounting of a slow but irreversible separation of Italian Socialism from Communist entanglement. In the past two years, it has begun to function as a constitutional "half party" opposition to Christian Democracy's dominance of public life.[3]

2. The Social Democrats' gains in the election of 1961 seem to have been due almost exclusively to the special circumstances of the Berlin crisis rather than to anything recognizably *Socialist* about their campaigning.

3. By the same process, the various lesser parties have tended either to wither away or to align themselves with the more independent elements among the Socialists.

In France, the advent of de Gaulle brutally upset the whole complicated checkerboard of party relationships. Traditional alignments and cleavages seemed lost in a monotonous uniformity of Gaullist allegiance. More recently, the outlines of a constitutional opposition have begun to appear. And once again, as in the other major countries of Western Europe, the chief elements of this opposition have been Socialist—whether it be the cautious and qualified anti-Gaullist stand of Guy Mollet's official Socialism or the far weaker but more militant "autonomous" Socialism of André Philip and Mendès-France. In either case, the evolution toward a one-and-a-half party situation has started.

How are we to explain a state of affairs in which conservative parties and movements have not only held on to power but enhanced that power for a decade and more? The event would not be so surprising if the social situation in the countries in question had been stable or only gradually altering. In fact, however, the past decade has seen very rapid economic and social changes. The great paradox of Western European society and politics is that the parties which apparently resist change are doing well while the parties with a vested ideological interest in change are doing badly.

Very briefly, what has been happening in Western Europe during the past few years has been a vast speed-up in a long-term shift toward a mobile, undifferentiated, and consumer-oriented society resembling that of the United States. The conservative parties have learned how to adjust to this change. Having come to power just as the great shift was beginning, they soon discovered ways to exploit the new social trends. They have accepted the welfare state; they have fostered the tendencies toward conformity that a mobile

society brings with it; they have systematically encouraged the corresponding turn from ideological and
political involvement—the apathy, the "privatization"
of life, the blurring of ideological distinctions, the
mounting suspicion that political debate is not very important, and the tendency to keep the larger public
issues from general discussion. Above all, the conservatives have known how to identify themselves with
the undeniable fact of economic prosperity.

In contrast, European Socialists have seemed disoriented and bewildered. Their political footwork has
been slower than that of the conservatives—indeed,
it is frequently the Socialists themselves whose instinc-
tive responses have appeared the more conservative of
the two. And it is true that the Socialist parties in
general have a longer and more continuous institutional history than the various conservative formations. On the Continent, the abrupt changes of regime
during the past half century, more particularly the experience of fascism and the Second World War, broke
up or demoralized the parties of the right; in Britain
alone there was no break in conservative continuity.
The Socialists, however—even when they were operating underground or in exile—never completely lost the
sense of a functioning political machine. In this respect,
their parties are the oldest and most routine-minded in
Europe. *As machines,* they are conservative by definition.

And yet, to pile on a counterparadox, the Socialists
alone seem able to muster a significant opposition
following. They may be functioning as only half a
party, but no other democratic opposition has been
able to win more than an insignificant fraction of the
electorate. Socialism may be old and unexciting, but it

offers the alternative that the politically disaffected naturally turn to when they want a change from conservative rule. All efforts to build progressive parties on a nonsocialist basis have failed, from Mendès-France's attempt in the mid 1950's to modernize the French Radical party to the constantly disappointed predictions that British Liberalism is about to make an electoral comeback. Mendès' eventual decision—after the advent of de Gaulle—to unite his shrunken forces with those of the Autonomous Socialists was an act of simple political realism. The opposition to conservative rule had to be socialist if it was to exist at all.

In trying to take account of this puzzling situation of semipermanent exclusion from power together with an unchallenged role as *the* constitutional opposition, the Socialist parties of Western Europe have proposed two widely contrasting solutions. They have agreed on the factual analysis of their plight. Nearly all discerning Socialists have recognized that the central practical problem for their parties is to break out of the confined circle of almost hereditary Socialist allegiance which on the Continent has restricted them to between 35 and 15 per cent of the vote.

This problem goes back as far as the 1890's, when a few far-seeing Socialists of strongly democratic loyalties, such as Eduard Bernstein, realized that the Marxian prediction of the proletariat's increasing to become the majority of mankind would never be realized; in advanced industrial societies, the percentage of factory hands would remain stable or actually fall—it was the white-collared and clerical, rather, whose numbers were rising. Hence a new type of appeal to reassure the peasantry and the small middle class was required. The succeeding decades brought no clear solution for this difficulty. Indeed, they intensified the earlier problems. The secession of the Communists after 1917 meant an irreplaceable loss from an already inadequate following. Postwar conditions pushed Socialist parties into power prematurely and without the parliamentary majority that was essential if they were actually to put their program into effect; government by Socialists in Germany in 1918 and 1928, in Britain in 1924 and 1929, and, most crucially, in France with the Popular Front government of 1936, brought disillusion rather than a sense of accomplishment—a loss rather than a reinforcement of popular following. But a full-scale re-examination of Socialist assumptions was never undertaken. It was not until the apparently far more favorable circumstances of the second postwar era had once again ended in disappointment that European Socialism began the examination of conscience that had been on its agenda for more than half a century.

The first (and more widely accepted) of the currently proposed solutions has been that of British Labour and the German Social Democrats. These have traditionally been the largest, the most influential, and the most conservative of European Socialist parties. In the autumn of 1959, both of them at last made explicit the departure from hallowed Socialist goals that had long underlain their day-to-day political activity. They virtually scrapped the standard central plank of all Socialist programs; they demoted the collectivization of the basic means of production—the nationalization of industry—from its position at the pinnacle of Socialist goals to a merely auxiliary (and unessential) status among a number of possible devices for economic control. They all but eliminated the idea of class struggle from their public pronouncements, and they aligned themselves unequivocally with the foreign policies of their national governments, pledging support for an alliance with the United States based on the protection of thermonuclear weapons.

In the two countries the ideological change differed markedly in tone and content. In Britain, the meeting at Blackpool was held in the shadow of the third of Labour's successive electoral defeats, and the mood was one of somber reflection on past errors. Moreover, the party was not fully united behind its official leaders, and Gaitskell and his allies did not obtain a clear-cut victory. Although at Blackpool Gaitskell staked his party leadership—and won—on his insistence that Labour repeal the clause in its party constitution pledging the eventual nationalization of all means of production, distribution, and exchange, he was subsequently obliged to accept a compromise formulation. And on foreign policy, the disaffection of the party's left wing counseled a similar caution; the storm was already brewing that in the following year seemed about to sweep Gaitskell himself from authority.

In the autumn of 1959, the German Social Democrats, midway between elections, were recovering confidence after their defeat two years earlier, and they were trying to put themselves in a good position for the election of 1961. Hence there was a bounce and aggressiveness about them which British Labour understandably lacked. Moreover, the Germans were troubled neither by a vociferous left wing nor by the memory of a period in power which had to be rationalized and defended. This was particularly important in the matter of nationalization. The German Social Democrats had never held national office since the Second World War;

they had not passed through British Labour's experience of actually carrying out a collectivist policy in the
half-decade immediately following the war; they did
not need to grapple with the British problem of whether
to renationalize those branches of the economy—notably steel and road transport—which the Tories had
subsequently returned to private ownership.

The German rejection of nationalization, then, was
less equivocal than the British. In its recognition of the
virtues of free enterprise, the new Social Democratic
program voted at Bad Godesberg rose to almost lyric
heights. "Competition as much as possible—planning
only as much as necessary" was a slogan calculated to
dismay the party faithful. To the uncommitted, on the
other hand, the program suggested moderation and
class reconciliation; it pledged a "new political style
of honesty, of objectivity, of cooperation, of synthesis."
And the following year, by its decision to pass over the
older party leaders and to present the young and
"dynamic" Willy Brandt as Social Democracy's candi-
date for the chancellorship, the party once again recognized the value of electoral sex appeal. It proposed
to take advantage of Brandt's position as mayor of
West Berlin in offering the public a Social Democratic
image of patriotism and orthodoxy in the cold war.

In France, Guy Mollett is apparently trying to lead
the larger wing of French Socialism along the same path
on which Gaitskell and Brandt have been moving in
Britain and in Germany. He agrees with them that
nationalization and class warfare should no longer be
emphasized and that the new respectability of European Socialism can be most profitably expressed
through giving bipartisan support to the Atlantic Pact.
He seems to believe, as Brandt and Gaitskell do, that

the way to adjust to the present European evolution toward an American type of society is to convert European Socialism into a catch-all welfare-state movement, with fluid ideological boundaries, rather like the Democratic party in the United States.

The alternative solution for resolving the Socialists' current difficulties is both less clear-cut and less influential than that proposed by Gaitskell, Brandt, and Mollet. Its chief proponents are the left wing of British Labour, the militantly oppositionist fraction of French Socialism that calls itself "autonomous" or "unified," and the majority organization of the Italian Socialist party. In Italy alone—for special reasons of history and temperament—this second body of opinion within European Socialism holds a predominant position.

The most arresting distinction between the Socialist left and the more powerful moderate current is on foreign and military policy. As opposed to the nearly unqualified support that the official leaders of British and German Socialism give to the foreign policy of Macmillan and Adenauer, the Socialist left is worried and disaffected. But it is far from clear about the substitute it would offer. While the majority of left Socialists argue for retention of the Atlantic alliance in modified form, some of the French are frank neutralists. The Italians for the most part restrict themselves to insisting on the purely defensive character of the Atlantic Pact and to opposing the stationing of American nuclear weapons on their country's soil. The British—drawing on the popular enthusiasm mobilized by the Campaign for Nuclear Disarmament—advocate Britain's unilateral renunciation of thermonuclear weapons and the closing down of American bases in Europe. In the autumn of 1960 they actually succeeded in winning a majority

in the party congress—until their position was reversed
by the votes of Labour members of Parliament who
remained loyal to Gaitskell. Yet for all its militancy,
British Labour's left wing does not always and invariably spurn the "defense umbrella" of nuclear retaliation
launched from the United States. Obviously this is a
question that it has not completely mastered. Throughout Western Europe, the logic of the left Socialist position is either a neutrality sympathetic to America or a
new type of Atlantic Pact pledged to defend Europe by
conventional weapons alone. But most of the adherents
of Socialism's left wing have not reached that far in
their thinking. While they argue that their countries'
present foreign policies are dangerous and mistaken,
they have not yet found an unambiguous substitute
for them.

On the domestic front, the lack of full-scale rethinking is at least as apparent. Most left Socialists are
unwilling to discard the old battle cries of nationalization and class warfare. But they have difficulty explaining why they feel that way. They suspect that men
like Gaitskell and Brandt are engaging in a "sell-out"
of traditional Socialism. At the same time, the better
economic heads among them have absorbed enough
of Keynes to have lost their faith in the panacea of
nationalization, and any honest left Socialist must recognize that class lines are far less sharp in Europe
today than they were a generation ago. Very often the
rhetoric of left Socialism boils down to little more than
an appeal for a return to first principles and a restoration of political militancy.

The Italian Socialists epitomize the confusion. For
half a century the Italians have ranked as the farthest
left of the major European Socialist parties. In its in-

sistence on class struggle—in its adherence to a "maximum" program—in its reluctance to make a clean break with Communism, the Italian party has reflected the peculiar social conditions of the slowest to develop and the least prosperous of the great nations of the West. In Italy, human misery of the nineteenth-century type is still a sharp reality. Quite understandably, its Socialists have reflected this condition by clinging to a nineteenth-century faith in proletarian solidarity and to a romantic vision of a new world of human brotherhood.

The Italian Socialist party carries around with it an enormous burden of past errors. It was the only great party that in the first postwar era tried to straddle the issue of affiliation with the Third International—the only branch of European Socialism whose majority failed to see the necessity of making a clear choice for or against the Bolshevik road to the future. After the Second World War, the Italian Socialists were equally blind to reality. Their decade and more of fellow traveling grievously eroded their moral capital, breeding a distrust among liberal-minded Italians which it will take at least another decade to efface. Yet for all this, there is something amazingly innocent about Italian Socialism. It has a quality of popular spontaneity that in other countries has quite disappeared from contemporary politics. Its trust in the future is of almost childlike intensity; it made its catastrophic mistakes in good faith. The new-old freshness of the Italian party offers a puzzling and still unexploited asset in European Socialism's current struggle for self-definition.

At first glance, it would seem that the British or the German solution—the path of Gaitskell or of

Brandt—has everything in its favor. In the short run, this is certainly true. It is undeniable that the European Socialist parties will not begin to win elections until they have convinced the middle-class electorate that they offer no real threat to private property or the prosecution of the cold war. They will not be within striking distance of power until they have converted themselves into welfare-state parties only marginally different from their conservative opponents. The evidence is overwhelming—at least in Britain—that a turn to the left would mean an almost automatic loss of Socialist votes.[4]

But is the current winning of elections the whole, or even the central, question? Even if Labour were to gain a parliamentary majority in Britain, or the Social Democrats should come to power in Germany, would they truly have solved their problem? History is full of examples of parties that have reached authority and then have lost power very rapidly, because they have not known how to behave once they were there. The defining characteristic of the Gaitskell-Brandt policy is what in this country used to be called "me-tooism." And the great weaknesses of "me-tooism" are its lack of political coherence and the fact that it is so easy a game for two to play. So long as European Socialists pursue this course, they can always be outflanked by an ideologically more supple conservative party.

It is only half true to say, as I did earlier, that nationalization of the basic means of production has traditionally been the major tenet of European socialism. This is true only in an instrumental sense; na-

4. See particularly the series of articles by Seymour Martin Lipset entitled "The British Voter," *The New Leader*, XLIII (November 7, 1960), 10-14; (November 21, 1960), 15-20; XLIV (February 6, 1961), 16-19.

tionalization has been the means, not the ultimate goal, of socialist policy. Indeed, this goal has not really been economic at all. It has been envisioned as a moral change—a transformation in the *quality* of life, from an absorption with private economic satisfactions to a concern for human personality and the well-being of the community as a whole.

This is the central point at issue between the dominant right and the uneasy left within the European Socialist parties. Here lie the true grounds for that suspicion of a sell-out on the part of men like Gaitskell and Brandt that the left has spotted so accurately but has seldom expressed with clarity. The official leadership of British and German Socialism is currently ready to settle for something way short of what European Socialists have always dreamed of. This is the real charge against the right—far more than its faltering on a merely technical question such as nationalization. The truly damning indictment that the left hurls at the right is its willingness to accept a society dedicated to private consumption, a politically and ideologically apathetic society, in which public goals are almost forgotten in the scramble for individual satisfactions. This we Americans know to be true of our own country. American society is democratic by almost any definition one might choose to propose —far more democratic than the societies of Britain and France and Germany and Italy have ever been. But it is also a smug and consumer-oriented society, in which private affluence is canceled out by public penury, and most of whose citizens lack a living faith in their own values.

Hence the European Socialists of the left are convinced that their own countries' transition to an American type of democracy is far from being a total blessing. Nearly all of them recognize that contemporary capitalism has vastly reduced the harshness and egoism of its nineteenth-century predecessor. At the same time, they argue that the new capitalism of the twentieth century, along with an unanticipated leveling of classes, has brought with it equally unanticipated evils of its own. This is what Aneurin Bevan, in one of his last major utterances as the eloquent spokesman of British Labour's left wing, meant when he declared that capitalism had *not* succeeded, that it had produced an ugly society in which values had "gone all wrong."

The Socialist left, then, is trying both to restore an old tradition of ideological affirmation and to adjust its goals to contemporary conditions, when it argues that in place of or alongside the conventional cure-all of nationalization, something more imaginative is required than mere adjustment to welfare-state capitalism. As opposed to the short-term "realism" of Socialism's right wing, it proposes such long-range measures as nationwide economic planning, a coherent public investment policy, and a vastly expanded program for raising the cultural level of the whole population. Such planning emphasizes "social priorities" for the entire community; the corresponding cultural policy stresses adult participation and development at least as much as formal schooling. It is characteristic of the "New Left," not only in Britain but on the Continent also, to criticize the present situation "in terms of moral and esthetic, rather than economic, criteria." Its "concern is above all with the impoverished quality of life . . . , the lack of a common culture, the decline of community, the dehumanizing effects of the mass media." [5] In this sense its manifestoes resemble such American works of social criticism as Paul Goodman's *Growing Up Absurd*. And the moral impetus behind them comes from a revulsion against the threat of thermonuclear destruction that is leading through a steady logical progression to neutralism or even the preaching of nonviolence in the Gandhian tradition.

But where does this leave the middle class? What do these noble aims have to do with the overriding practical question of breaking out of half a generation of conservative dominance and winning over a new segment of the electorate? The answer is that the Socialist left is taking a long gamble on the future. It is convinced that the policy of the Gaitskells and the Brandts is myopic and, in the end, self-defeating. Ultimately, it believes, a mere consumers' paradise will prove disappointing. A thirst for Utopia will reawaken everywhere. Finally this longing will reach the middle class itself. Or rather—since the familiar class lines will have broken down so profoundly—dissatisfaction with the consumer society will become diffused throughout the population. Then the old moral message of European Socialism will come to have a new relevance. And those parties and groups which have maintained through countless checks and errors their utopian aspirations undimmed, will find themselves no longer marginal half-parties in a sterile and electorally hopeless political debate, but leaders and mentors of a great ideological reawakening.

5. Lewis Coser, "Socialism and Apathy," *Dissent*, VIII (Winter, 1961), 25.

CHAPTER 8

How Democratic Is Christian Democracy?

In any assessment of the political prospects for Western Europe, Christian Democracy necessarily takes a central place. Its present prominence offers the great ideological novelty of the postwar era—considerably more of a novelty than the strength of Communism, which was already anticipated in the interwar period. The fact that political parties inspired by Christian principles hold around a third of the seats in the lower houses of Western and Central European parliaments— and that a *majority* of those deputies loyal to the Western concept of liberty call themselves Christian Democrats—suggests the extent of this postwar growth. Among European ideologies of the mid-century, Christian Democracy is both the most pervasive and the most difficult to define.

Catholic apologists customarily *assume* the compatibility of Christianity and democracy.[1] They do not argue it—they just beg the whole question. Historically, however, I think it is beyond dispute that democracy

1. See, for example, Michael P. Fogarty, *Christian Democracy in Western Europe, 1820-1953* (Notre Dame, Ind.: University of Notre Dame Press, 1957).

on the Western European Continent grew up outside of and frequently in opposition to the tradition of organized Christianity. Things were quite different in Britain and in the United States, but on the Continent the characteristic democratic leadership until comparatively recently was at the very least secular-minded, agnostic, or anticlerical if not frankly anti-Christian— "humanist" rather than religious in inclination.

In passing over or minimizing this traditional cleavage, Christian Democracy's defenders have found it useful to concentrate on the social as opposed to the political groupings within the movement as a whole. In the worthy endeavors of labor, youth, and family organizations, a kind of Boy Scout morality offers a convenient link between the mentality of the religious and that of the secular-oriented: where the major goals are tangible and precise, final philosophical issues may well remain obscure. In national politics it is otherwise. Here—again I am speaking only of the European Continent—ideology is central: ultimately the great divisive issues cannot be denied.

Moreover, by focusing on social organizations at the expense of politics, the apologists of Christian Democracy accomplish another feat of subtle readjustment. In youth and family groups, Christian Democratic principles can appear in their "purest" and most attractive guise; in politics they reveal all the insufficiencies of practical and worldly compromise. Indeed, it is in the Christian Democratic political parties that we first discern the enormous gap between principle and practice characteristic of movements of this sort. Such is most notably the case with the two great parties that have governed West Germany and Italy without interruption over the past decade and a half. From the regimes established by Adenauer and De Gasperi the general public has derived its conception of what Christian Democracy is all about. In terms of Catholic apologetics, this may be unfortunate. But it cannot be altered simply by a unilateral declaration that politics is a secondary matter in the Christian Democratic hierarchy of values.

By their position as virtual monopolists of governmental authority, the Christian Democratic parties of Germany and Italy have perforce been drastically altered in character. The consolidation of their situation as the exclusive wielders of administrative power has been at the expense of their traditional principles. Where these called for decentralization and "vertical pluralism," the actual conduct of government in Germany and Italy has emphasized central authority and the power of the state. In Italy in particular, the governing party's conviction of its own indispensability in the struggle against Communism has served to justify a multitude of sins. Again and again the party has revealed a guilty penchant for indirect censorship and thought control. And along with these has gone a notable reinforcement of clerical influence.

Christian Democracy over the past fifteen years has epitomized a new political phenomenon—the emergence of *governmental* parties within the Continental democratic tradition. This is by no means the same as what has been called a *state* party, with reference to single-party systems of the Communist or fascist type. Nor does it correspond to the situation of traditional liberal parties that have succeeded in maintaining themselves in power for a quarter-century at a stretch: in the nineteenth century, the long periods of dominance on the part of the Liberals or Conservatives in England,

and of the Republicans in the United States, were less thoroughgoing in their effects on the dominant parties themselves, since control of the state machine gave them less extensive powers than is the case today.

The position of the American Democratic party between 1933 and 1953 comes closer to the definition I am suggesting. The record of the Roosevelt and Truman administrations in coping with depression and with wars hot and cold, and in expanding the bureaucratic apparatus, meant that within the party's ranks, and even to a large extent within the permanent civil service, the conviction grew that the Democrats alone were sufficiently responsible and competent to conduct the business of government. To these people, a Republican victory represented not only a political disaster but, from the administrative standpoint, a perilous leap into the unknown; hence the near-panic of a large number of essentially conservative civil servants at Eisenhower's election in 1952.

On the Continent during the postwar period, a similar conviction of the administrative indispensability of a single party established itself in a more thoroughgoing fashion. And understandably so, since the Christian Democratic parties of Italy and West Germany were called on to cope with problems even graver than those that had confronted the Roosevelt administration in the United States—nothing less than the whole reconstruction of the state apparatus, the re-establishment of a respect for legal procedures, and a restoration of confidence in the traditional governing elites. Entirely independently, then, of the political and religious ideologies they espoused, such heads of government as De Gasperi and Adenauer became associated in their own and in the public mind with the state authority itself. And their association with the United States gave a further official stamp to the parties they led.

This quasi-official character of the Christian Democratic parties of Italy and Germany brought mixed benefits both to the parties themselves and to the nations they governed. The impression of "soundness" and of American backing they exuded naturally provoked dissatisfaction—which was only intensified by the ineptitude with which American diplomatic spokesmen underlined the obvious in distributing gratuitous electoral advice. By the same token, these parties were obliged to take their electoral stand essentially on the success of the nation's economic recovery—which in itself was sufficient to explain their triumphant progress in Germany and their more spotty parliamentary showing in Italy. And, rather more significantly, their position as governmental parties was consolidated at the expense of their Christian Democratic character. In Italy at least, the boundaries between bureaucracy and party became increasingly blurred, and the spoils system began to acquire connotations of an overriding reason of state. The lack of any apparent alternative to Christian Democratic rule gave the sanction of expediency to minor corruption, administrative arbitrariness, and the betrayal or watering down of programatic commitments. As time went on, the position of both the Italian and the German Christian Democratic parties as *the* government party became more significant than either their politico-religious ideology or their social composition.

Here we find a further example of the way in which the Communist problem has limited political action in our time to a choice of more or less unpalatable al-

ternatives. And this is true both for the governmental
party itself and for the electorate: the latter is reduced
to casting its vote in a negative and skeptical spirit;
the former is saddled with an electoral following that
has no interest in its professed principles. At the
same time, there is a species of logic in this unhappy
union between party and electorate: a right-center,
socially unhomogeneous, and covertly clerical political
movement is well suited to provide the peculiar ideological amalgam that fits the public temper of the present time—a conservatism softened by welfare-state procedures, an anti-Communist militancy whose moral
vigor is undercut by civic slackness, an insistence on
personal liberty that is constantly belied by the official
encouragement of intellectual and spiritual conformity.

In broader terms, the fact that Christian Democracy
in its lower ranks is so often ethically attractive and
at its more exalted levels is correspondingly depressing
is similarly no accident of circumstance. It is implicit,
rather, in the underlying character of Christian Democracy itself. In its junior ranks, Christian Democracy
includes many of the most devoted younger activists
that Western Europe currently affords. At the top, its
leaders are all too often routine politicians—and sanc-
timonious ones to boot.

Why is this the case? Initially it is worth noting that
in Christian Democracy, the second term of the title is
instrumental to the first. A Christian Democrat is a
Christian primarily, and a democrat only in a subordinate capacity. The adjective is more important than
the noun. In Social Democracy it is just the reverse:
the behavior of European Socialists during the past
forty years has demonstrated that in their eyes the

interests of democracy override those of socialism. In this second case, since both the terms of loyalty are terrestrial, a choice can be reached through a rational weighing of the relevant issues. For Christian Democrats, on the other hand, no real choice exists: since one term is spiritual and the other political, it is obvious which takes precedence.

It is for this reason that the behavior of Christian Democratic parties offers such a bewildering alternation of moral judgments and opportunist calculation, and why their policy has been assessed so very differently by their apologists and by their detractors. For the former, the Christian Democrats are living examples of morality in action; for the latter, they shift their principles to every change in the political weather. Both evaluations are in one or another sense correct. Christian Democrats quite natually feel called upon to make moral judgments in nearly every sphere of life —but since the criterion of these judgments is religious rather than political, an opportunist selection of political *means* to moral *ends* may at the same time appear perfectly permissible. Such is the more disquieting significance of that ideological flexibility in which Christian Democrats take particular pride.

In a peaceful era, this discrepancy creates no serious difficulty. But in times of civil tension, it may bring enormous political hazards. When religion itself appears threatened, the Christian Democrat faces a painful choice. To save his religious faith, he may be obliged to sacrifice his political principles—to preserve Christianity from godless revolution, he may feel it necessary to jettison democracy and have recourse to authoritarian government. Such was the logic of the vote of full powers that the Christian Democrats of

Italy and Germany gave first to Mussolini, and a decade later to Hitler—a practical application of the well-tried Catholic principle of submitting to a lesser evil in order to ward off one greater. Both parties later regretted the stand they had taken, but too late to undo what they had helped to accomplish.

I recall these "old, unhappy, far-off things" not in a spirit of anticlerical provocation, but rather to rectify an impression that is widespread in the United States today. A majority of Americans are apparently convinced that there is some ineradicable insufficiency in the agnostic or "humanist" view of democracy. The religious interpretation of democratic principles is becoming increasingly common in our country. All manner of public leaders, from our presidents down, have suggested in no uncertain terms that it is difficult to be a good democrat (or American) if one is not a good Christian (or Jew). To such an equation an unrepentant agnostic or "humanist" must necessarily object with all the vigor at his command. In historical terms, the argument is preposterous. In terms of contemporary politics, it is dangerously discriminatory. Indeed, the reverse can be argued rather more convincingly. To agnostics, democracy is not instrumental to some otherworldly goal—it is a terrestrial benefit in its own right, subordinate to no other.

Thus the central point of the controversy between the apologists and the critics (like myself) of Christian Democracy is in the view each holds of the last century and a half of European history. Both can agree that in the past thirty or forty years a new definition of democracy has emerged on the European Continent and that this new view is more liberal in the best sense, more tolerant of the rights of minorities, than its "Jacobin" predecessor. But the Christian Democrats and their critics differ in their respective notions of how and under whose auspices the change came about. Moreover, we who are critical of Christian Democracy discern the outlines of a third phase of European democratic history—a phase of resurgent clericalism—that is superseding the second phase of mutual tolerance between Catholics and unbelievers. Christian Democracy's apologists deny (if only by implication) the very existence of this third phase: they see different persecutors and different persecutees from those we do. Who is currently provoking whom, who currently has the upper hand, as between the religious and the unbelievers—that is the nub of the question.

I would not ascribe, as Catholic apologists do, the more tolerant attitude among democrats that emerged on the European Continent after the First World War primarily or even substantially to the activities of Christian political leaders. As I see it, the Christian Democratic parties and movements reflected or profited by, rather than brought about, a change that was *already* occurring in the breasts of their agnostic adversaries. And this change was becoming apparent even before the outbreak of the First World War. Not too long after the turn of the century, secular-minded prime ministers, such as Giolitti in Italy or Briand in France, were beginning to mitigate the rigors of anticlericalism in their respective countries. The way was already being prepared for the acceptance of Christian Democracy as an equal partner in the European democratic tradition.

Why was this the case? I do not believe that it was so much because of anything the Christian Democrats themselves had said or done—although, as we shall

see in a moment, this latter had its importance also—
as on account of a vast change in the political situation
itself. By 1913, in a formal sense at least, the battle
for democracy on the Western European Continent
had substantially been won. The German Empire alone
was still holding out against the democratic onslaught:
nearly everywhere else parliamentary regimes based
on universal manhood suffrage had become the rule.
And with the triumph of electoral democracy the political power of the Catholic Church had been broken:
the clerical danger that once had offered the rallying
cry for democratic politicians had lost its immediacy.

Of course I have simplified the story greatly. But the
point I should like to stress is that, just at the moment
when the Christian Democratic leaders were giving
irrefutable proof of their democratic sincerity—just at
the time when they were in a position to guarantee to
any fair-minded person that the old equation between
religion and reaction no longer necessarily held true—
at this very point the secular-minded (who still dominated the political scene) were already engaged in a
substantial revision of their earlier attitude. Naturally
the liberals and the radicals seldom said in so many
words that they were abandoning their anticlerical positions: to do so would have been politically inadvis-
able—the old slogans were still the most reliable for
electoral purposes. But *in practice* they had come a
long way from the "priest-eating" paroxysms of *le
petit père* Combes.[2]

At the same time, this new tolerance for religious
values in political life was not granted unconditionally.

2. The Prime Minister of France (1902-1905) who was responsible for the abrogation of the Concordat with the Catholic
Church.

It was granted on the understanding that the tolerance would be reciprocal—that the religious-minded would not seek to impose *their* values on the "humanists" and the unbelievers in the fashion in which the latter had once tried to impose an agnostic philosophy on the religious. If in the second quarter of the twentieth century so many liberals and radicals (and, eventually, even socialists) came to admit that their former efforts had been mistaken—if they were prepared to wink at evasions of the laws against the holding of property by religious bodies and to give tacit approval to the reopening of Church schools on a vast scale—it was because they believed that clericalism was a thing of the past. The implied corollary to the new attitude of tolerance among secular-minded democrats was a similar attitude on the part of the religious. Only the conviction that Christian Democracy rather than clericalism would soon be the dominant ideology among Western European Christians (and more particularly among Catholics) made possible the second phase of European democratic development.

Then the unexpected happened: clericalism revived. This is the third phase whose outlines are only just beginning to become clear. In the years since 1945, clericalism has proved that it is far from dead—but it has changed its form and its modes of action in such a way as to make it difficult to recognize (particularly for those of genuine Christian Democratic conviction). Briefly, what has happened is that the clerical attitude has revived *within* the Christian Democratic movements. Under the sheltering umbrella of parties ostensibly hostile to Church interference in political life, clericalism has once again become a threat to the European democratic tradition.

It was all very well when Christian Democracy con-
sisted of minority movements, still battling their way
for recognition as equals. Under those circumstances
there was no particular attraction for the nondemo-
cratic or the clerical-minded to climb aboard. But after
Adenauer and De Gasperi made their parties the dominant force within their respective nations, the temptation to participate in the Catholic victory became overwhelming. Thousands of new recruits flocked to the
majority party—recruits whose democratic convictions
were only verbal and whose true loyalties lay in the
sacristy.

There was also an important difference between generations. De Gasperi and men of his age and type were
liberals by conviction, rooted in the parliamentary tradition, men who had tempered their democratic faith
in the fire of fascist oppression. And—to take the case
of Italy again, which is the most familiar to me and
also, perhaps, the most important—they had gone
through the searing experience of disavowal by the
Pope himself.[3] The younger leaders came from quite
different origins: *their* youth had been passed under
fascism, they had never had a chance to participate in
parliamentary life, and the mentality of the authoritarian state had left its traces upon them. By conscious
conviction they became antifascists, but in their habitual mental responses they still betray the influence of
the atmosphere of official paternalism and corporative
economics in which they grew up.

I can cite as evidence a book by the Italian Christian
Democratic leader Dino del Bo.[4] In Italy, Del Bo ranks

3. In 1923, one year after Mussolini's accession to power.
4. *Italian Catholics in Crisis* (Milwaukee, Wis.: Marquette
University Press, 1957).

as one of the main hopes of the reforming wing of Christian Democracy. He is certainly a man attuned to the contemporary world, well aware that the overriding imperative for his party is to win away the industrial and agrarian workers from their Communist allegiance. Yet his general approach is not exactly liberal: his preference for corporative solutions to economic problems and his distaste for secular democracy are all too evident; he is obviously impatient for the day when his party can get along without its present vestigial remnants of secular alliances. Through the vague and wordy phraseology of his book, the vision of the future that emerges is of a vast union of spirits—a paternalistic Catholic state dedicated to the welfare of the laboring masses.

Del Bo's essay suggests the cardinal error that so many outsiders make in assessing the current trends within Christian Democracy, both in Italy and elsewhere. Taking their cue from the "Modernist" period of the early part of this century, they equate social reform with liberalism, and these in turn with latitudinarianism in dogma, describing all three in terms of a Catholic "left." Around 1905, such was indeed the case; liberalism in politics, a sympathy for the peasants and workers, and a "Modernist" interpretation of dogma generally went hand in hand. Today this is far from true; indeed, as in Del Bo's case, the younger and reform-minded leaders are frequently the more authoritarian in their general approach to politics. And when they describe themselves in terms of a Catholic "left," it is not necessarily Christian dogma they have in mind. In dogmatic matters, the young social reformers may well be more uncompromising and orthodox than their elders.

Thus, as I see it, the present danger of a new clerical-ism exists in two forms, which, despite their ostensible hostility to each other, are in fact mutually reinforcing. The first and more obvious form is the penetration of Christian Democratic movements by conservatives whose true sentiments are more clerical than demo-cratic. The second and more subtle form is the evolu-tion of so many younger Christian Democratic leaders, only half-consciously and often against their announced intention, toward a position that in reality if not in name is similarly clerical.

One's judgment of this new phenomenon naturally depends on the perspective and life situation from which one starts. Christian Democratic apologists, with their eyes fixed on the "heartland" of fervent Catholi-cism extending from the Netherlands through the Rhineland to the Alps and Venice, view the emerging third phase of European democratic development in positive terms, in terms of a new fellowship arising out of Christian movements that are more social than po-litical—in terms of a "breakthrough" beyond the con-stituency of church-goers to a wider gathering-in and reconciliation of whole populations to Christian values. I, with my experience rooted in Italy—and in Massa-chusetts—see something more threatening: an *imposi-tion* of Christian values on a secular or "humanist" minority. And in justifying my own stand, I think it worth recalling that Italy shelters the headquarters of world Catholicism and that Massachusetts is the strong-hold of Catholicism in the United States. As a citizen of the latter state, I must necessarily protest against the clerically-inspired measures that seek not only to limit our reading and the films we are permitted to see but also to impose on us the Catholic view of the proper size of families.

The same reasoning can be applied to more strictly political arguments. I would certainly not try to deny the plain fact that in Italy and in Germany—and, to an extent, even in France—Christian Democracy took the lead in supporting the values of freedom in the trying postwar years. I would also agree that the results of this labor were more positive than negative. But I refuse to grant that the passing of the initiative to Christian Democracy betokened any radical deficiency on the part of the secular democratic parties. The former simply had more votes—and I do not have to remind the religious that God is not necessarily on the side of the big battalions. Indeed, I might even argue that in the first important postwar turn toward authoritarianism on the Western European Continent, secular democracy proved rather more sure of its own values than did the democrats of Christian inspiration. The coming to power of de Gaulle was not strictly comparable to the advent of Mussolini or of Hitler—but there were important points of resemblance. Once again, in the vote of investiture of June 1, 1958, Christian Democracy simply folded up—as it had done before in 1922 and in 1933. It was Radicals and Socialists who provided nearly all the democratic votes of opposition.

Thus, when Christian Democratic apologists propose to balance off Franco and Salazar against Khrushchev and Tito, as parallel examples of Catholic and of atheist dictators, I think they are neglecting an important distinction. Franco and Salazar, however much democratic Catholics may hate them, share the latters' religious faith; Khrushchev and Tito have a faith at variance with my own and that of the overwhelming majority of secular-minded democrats. The leaders of the Soviet Union and of Yugoslavia, in theory at least, are Marxists; their opposite numbers in the Socialist parties of Western and Central Europe are not. In broader terms, we "humanists" are in a position to disavow Khrushchev and Tito in a more thoroughgoing fashion than is possible in the case of democratic Catholics and their Iberian coreligionists. I do not claim that we agnostics are more virtuous than the believers— the contrary may well be the case. I simply claim that we are freer—freer to admit our errors and to change our minds. And one of the greatest admissions of error of the present century has been the abandonment of dogmatic Marxism on the part of the European Socialists and on the part of so many secular-minded Americans of my own generation.

We humanists are sure of very few things—and most of these are certain rather simple ethical precepts on which we follow in the Judeo-Christian tradition. Generally we are not at all sure what the right course of political action may be. But we have a fairly good idea of the course that is radically wrong—and by that I hope it is quite clear that I mean the procedures pursued by Khrushchev or Franco. On these fundamentals there is no disagreement between Christian Democrats and democrats of a secular turn of mind. Within the limits of such a consensus, the widest latitude of political alliance is both possible and essential: both sides can agree that the tragedy of the Fourth French Republic—as of Italy from 1919 to 1922— lay in the failure of Christian Democrats and Socialists to reach a common program of social reconstruction.

Beyond this minimum of agreement—beyond the basic ethical principles we hold in common—Catholics and secularists necessarily diverge. Where the Church itself is concerned, where clericalism, new or old, enters the scene, each side must be on its guard. I like Giolitti's classic definition of Church and state as parallel lines that should never meet. For when they do, explosions are bound to occur. To avoid such explosions in a period of clerical resurgence—Protestant as well as Catholic—requires something more than the polite looking the other way that has become *de rigueur* in American politics. It requires a willingness to speak out—even at the risk of wounding one's best friends.

As I write these final lines, my conscience smites me. Face after face rises before my eyes—of good men, of fair-minded men, tolerant and sympathetic to a fault, a gallant minority clinging loyally to their faith despite the obstacles that stubborn leaders of the hierarchy and ignorant parish priests strew along their path. These are the Catholics I know: a *real* Christian Democrat in France, a group of young historical scholars in my own country, a "Jansenist" in Rome tirelessly reminding Italy's self-styled Christian government of its true moral responsibilities. The majority of their co-religionists may well suspect my friends of heresy. These latter know that it is love for their Church and respect for its tradition that lead them to question its inflexibility. My hopes are with them in their lonely struggle.

CHAPTER 9

Gaullism in the
Mirror of History

AMONG THE various anecdotes, authentic or *bien trou-vées,* that circulated in Paris in the summer of 1958, the one that best expressed the country's perplexities ran as follows. An old friend of de Gaulle's, not currently associated with the government, came to call on the new Prime Minister; on taking his leave, he was amazed to find André Malraux, reputed to be de Gaulle's closest collaborator, literally throwing himself upon him with the anxious query, "You who know the General so well, tell me, what does he really think?"

During the three months between the installation of de Gaulle's government in late May and the announcement of the new constitution in early September, the whole of France was asking itself the same question. The revolutionary change had been accomplished— what the political experts had dismissed as impossible had in fact occurred—yet the outlines of the new regime were far from clear. The country was living suspended between two eras, with the Fourth Republic obviously dead but the Fifth still to be defined. In Paris the commissions elaborating the new institutions and the new policy worked long and earnestly—no holidays for them. The rest of the French elite simply went off on vacation.

It was a strange and most unrevolutionary atmosphere. There was as little apparent enthusiasm as there was militant or organized protest; the dominant mood was acceptance tinged with anxiety. In the dead weeks that extended from the Fourteenth of July—a holiday celebrated that year with unprecedented official orchestration and expense—to the beginning of the autumn electoral season, the French held their breath and hoped for the best. Their fate, they knew, had been taken out of their hands. With all other possibilities foreclosed, they had played their last card. And the most disquieting thing was that nobody knew exactly what this card was worth.

All the obvious parallels and precedents were inapplicable. The American journalists who found reassurance in de Gaulle and pictured him as the restorer of orderly administration, might be as far astray as the Italians, who quite understandably, in terms of their own experience, compared him to Mussolini. Both simplified an enormously complex situation. All that was clear to everybody was that the French had entrusted themselves to a *man*—rather than to an idea, an institution, or a party. In this situation, a "cult of personality" was unavoidable, however distasteful it might be to the majority of Frenchmen. Or—to quote Malraux's Fourteenth of July declaration—"Some want the Republic without General de Gaulle, as others want . . . de Gaulle without the Republic. But France . . . wants the Republic *with* . . . de Gaulle." As an ideological definition for the vacation season, that had to suffice.

Thus any effort to place the new dispensation, to situate the France of de Gaulle in political and historical perspective, must start with an assessment of the General himself. Even this narrower task has its inextricable complexities. For de Gaulle as a historical figure has appeared in two quite different capacities: his original bright image is blurred with a second image of more doubtful character. From 1940 to 1945, he was the lone fighter for freedom, the man who gradually succeeded in rallying to his cause the vast majority of the public-spirited and the politically articulate— and thereby restored to the French people their national self-esteem. Two years later, however, he reappeared as the leader of a faction, a political partisan who, under the guise of reuniting the French, in fact divided them still further. This second effort ended in failure. But its highly checkered existence altered beyond recognition the original meaning of the terms "Gaullism" and "Gaullist." In the war and resistance years, these had come to suggest a militant republicanism—a spirit and a constituency that were quasi-socialist in character. After 1947, Gaullism was distinctly a movement of the right, with a large proportion of its adherents drawn from the former following of Pétain. By 1953, when the General gave his followers their "freedom of action" and withdrew from the leadership of his Rally of the French People, little seemed left of his original reputation and prestige. In this perspective, his triumphant return five years later was all the more surprising.

Fortunately for his historical repute (and for the peace of mind of those who seek to understand him) he occupied the half decade of his retirement with the composition of three stout volumes of memoirs. From

them there emerges once again a figure of large dimensions—of a stubborn consistency through all his
changes of following and fortune. A few very simple
ideas, we see, have been the mainsprings of his conduct. And these are notably archaic: a concept of
France as a nation of special excellence and with a
special "mission," a view of the French as a people
who can be led by "dreams," above all a notion of
"grandeur"—the word is the *leitmotif* of his whole
book. When "grandeur" fails, we gather, then life is
scarcely worth living.

But this is not all. There is also de Gaulle the expert
in tank warfare, the young officer driving hard for the
technical improvement of his army. There is the de
Gaulle who can share with his socialist counsellors the
vision of a new France of social justice. In short, there
is de Gaulle the modern man. In his memoirs he appears as a Churchillian figure, temperamentally a
survival of the old regime, but sufficiently intelligent to
be aware of the technical needs of an industrial world.
As in Churchill's case, however, this awareness takes
second rank; de Gaulle is not really interested in economic problems. For him, the modernization of France
is a subsidiary concern; social reform, technical improvement—these are simply means to a greater goal.
Again it is the "grandeur" of his country that is pri-
mary.

Yet surely one can doubt whether the grandeur of
France is compatible with its industrial modernization.
It is far from clear that one can reconcile a nostalgia
for past glories with an adjustment to the contemporary
world. This is the central problem confronting the
Gaullist experiment.

*   *   *

It was as a lone individual without an organized
movement or party that de Gaulle came to power in
the spring of 1958. His wartime followers had scattered
in a hundred directions; only fragments remained of
his Rally of the French People. At the start of the May
crisis, no more than a handful of deputies saw him as
a possible solution. By the end of the month, he received a massive vote of confidence. This sequence of
events already presented an enormous riddle. In the
absence of other guideposts, the manner of de Gaulle's
coming to power suggested an initial characterization
of his regime.

In a technical sense, the advent of de Gaulle was
legal and constitutional. In real terms, it was not. (We
may recall that Mussolini and Hitler similarly came
to power under technically constitutional auspices.)
Lacking organized support in France itself, de Gaulle
was enabled to come to power *solely* through the
threat of force from Algiers. The North African *coup
d'état* of May 13 created a situation which he alone
was in a position to resolve. Hence the deputies had
no true freedom of choice: they were *forced* to vote
for de Gaulle—or to face the consequences. These
consequences, however, were not precisely what the
press took them to be. It was not the threat of civil war
or a Popular Front that drove the deputies to vote the
investiture; scarcely anyone was prepared to take up
arms for the Fourth Republic, and the Popular Front
was never a real possibility. It was simply and brutally
the fear of a parachute attack from Algiers.

All this may be obvious—but in the euphoria of the
succeeding months it was something that tended to be
forgotten. De Gaulle came in, not on a wave of enthusiasm, but in the cold chill of fear. As one wag summa-

rized the situation: "Caught between red terror and white terror, France was scared blue." There was nothing glorious about it—no trace of grandeur here. In their minds, the deputies could already see the "paras" slogging down the Champs Elysées—as they did in fact on the following Fourteenth of July, to the applause of a delighted throng. And even the courageous band among the non-Communist left who voted against de Gaulle's investiture did so with an eye more to their historical reputations than to any practical result. Everyone wanted to be among the immortal "eighty"—a reference to those who in 1940 had voted against Pétain. But they did not want the eighty to swell to too large a number: even *they* knew in their hearts that there was no alternative to de Gaulle.

Yet this was a solution which very few preferred in the abstract. Such was the paradox of the Gaullist "revolution." It was a revolution almost without partisans—except for the elegant young men who honked their horns in cadence as they drove their expensive cars around the Etoile. Sometime back about 1950 there had been talk of a "Gaullism without de Gaulle." Now, quite unexpectedly, in May, 1958, France had de Gaulle without Gaullism. For even the junta in Algiers had put forward his candidacy as a second best. The *colons,* at least, would have preferred someone more uncompromisingly authoritarian and conservative. Thus from the very moment of his investiture de Gaulle was able to present himself in the role he preferred, as an arbiter above party. In this sense he succeeded in returning to his wartime image—in transcending the partisan memory that his Rally of the French People had left behind it.

At the same time there was more than accident—

and another wartime memory—in the fact that the original impulse behind the new regime had come from Algiers. For the first time in history the French Empire had imposed its will on the home country. And the fact that this was possible was itself a legacy of the war period and of the personal initiative of de Gaulle. From 1940 to 1944, Free France had been largely an imperial, an African affair. It had established its first solid territorial base at Brazzaville; it was from the Chad that Leclerc began the spectacular advance north across the Sahara that brought the Free French forces into the main theater of combat; and Algiers provided the temporary capital for the provisional government that was eventually to assume power at home.

De Gaulle's wartime thinking was consciously and proudly imperial (again a Churchillian parallel). Among the charges he makes in his memoirs against "defeatists" such as Weygand and Pétain, one of the most important is their failure to think in imperial terms, to see the possibilities of further resistance beyond the limits of Continental France. And when at last de Gaulle was proved right, when he entered Paris in triumph in August, 1944, he brought the French Empire with him. This was a dubious gift at best. For it meant that postwar France, unlike Germany or Italy, would be unable to devote all its energies to reconstruction at home. There would always be the obsession of the Empire, the agonizing drain of colonial warfare.

The Fourth Republic did not collapse because of anything it did or failed to do at home—although its record there was mediocre enough. Had there been no Empire left, had France been in the situation of Germany or Italy, it could doubtless have muddled along with its existing institutions. Its failure came on the question of the colonies, and more particularly on the question of Algeria. For those who love paradox, there may be a bitter satisfaction in recognizing that de Gaulle came to power precisely because the burden with which he himself had saddled his country—the burden of imperial grandeur—had finally become too heavy to bear.

Once installed in power, the new regime had to supply itself with some sort of ideological equipment. The product of this necessity was much fumbling and a minimum of clear definition. But as early as the summer of 1958 the rough lines of an ideological pedigree were beginning to emerge. The French, after all, are a history-minded people, and every French regime since 1814 has tried to anchor itself in some earlier historical experience. By 1958, however, most of these precedents from the past had worn themselves out. For the new rulers of the French nation, the range of ideological choice was narrow in the extreme.

Just as the successive collapses of 1940 and 1958 had discredited the formula of parliamentary democracy, so the Vichy experience had made impossible any direct evocation of authoritarian conservatism. Indeed, that had been the trouble with the earlier Rally of the French People. Although such was far from de Gaulle's intent, the Rally smacked too much of Vichy. Or—on the other horn of the dilemma—its elected representatives tended to become ordinary parliamentarians in the conservative republican tradition. It was in this fashion that the Rally had finally fallen apart. Its failure offered a warning to all good Gaullists in their third and most decisive incarnation.

This time the very lack of an organized movement

had distinct advantages. It served as a persuasive answer to the charge that the new Gaullism was in any conscious sense fascist in inspiration. And it made possible the most extraordinary improvisations and adaptations. In his government as originally constituted, de Gaulle seemed to have picked his ministers almost at random. Along with a large number of civil servants and "technicians," one found the two most influential parliamentarians of the Assembly that had just been sent home in disgrace—Pinay for the right, Mollet for the left. It was as though in his disdainful *grand seigneur* manner, de Gaulle had decided that the whole issue was not particularly important, that he could pick his colleagues from where he wished, including the debris of the old political parties. Moreover, these were not really to be his colleagues: they were to be clerks or servants. The ministry did not function as a true cabinet with joint responsibility. Indeed, one indiscreet participant—Malraux again—went so far as to describe an early session as "similar to those in Napoleon's time."

In the first weeks of the new regime, the despatch of official business proceeded at a Napoleonic pace. In his highly personal style that combined majesty with elusiveness, de Gaulle gave orders and his harassed ministers did their best to carry them out. Or rather, they were harassed in a different and perhaps less taxing manner than had been the case in the past. The telephones in their offices had stopped ringing; a great calm settled over the ministries, as the deputies and senators ceased their customary importunities. For the first time in living memory, the higher civil servants observed, it was possible to put in a full day's work almost without interruption.

The historical image is of France in 1800—Bonaparte is First Consul, and, after the shabbiness and corruption of half a decade of rule by committee, the country has at last found a master capable of putting the administrative machine in order. But this master is still only Citizen Bonaparte: he is not yet Emperor. Republican forms have been preserved, the effete heirs of the great Revolution have been absorbed into the new administration, and a margin of liberty remains. The memory of the heroic, embattled Republic of 1793 is still fresh—but it is a memory that the First Consul is seeking to discipline and to steer into constructive channels.

Substitute the wartime resistance for 1793, and the Fourth Republic for the Directory, and you have a suggestion of the ideological atmosphere in which the Fifth Republic was launched. It evoked Bonapartism in its "pure" and truly popular form, before it was overladen with the flummeries of the Napoleonic Empire. This is a Bonapartism with which most Americans are unfamiliar, and which even for the French has become dimmed by successive deformations. When we think today of the heirs of Napoleon, our minds turn toward more sinister things—the association of the military with royalism and reaction, the persecution of Captain Dreyfus, and the fascist agitation of the 1930's. Since the turn of the century, at least, nationalism in the Napoleonic tradition has appeared most often as the sworn enemy of republican and democratic institutions.

Yet this was not always or necessarily so. Throughout the past century and a half of French history, there has never ceased to exist an alternative possibility, the thin thread of a contrary tradition, often scarcely perceptible but never completely submerged. Within this alternative tradition, democracy and the Republic have figured as perfectly compatible with militarism and strong government. Such were the perspectives which Napoleon himself sought to provide in the proclamations of his Hundred Days. And in thus returning to his own ideological origins, he set the stage for the development of a personal legend that was at variance with the imperial phase of his career, and for the association of Bonapartism with Jacobinism in the 1820's and 1830's. In this lay the basis of Napoleon III's popular appeal: when, in his imprecise and rambling style, he wrote of the "Napoleonic ideas" that he proposed to incarnate, democracy and equality naturally took a prominent place among them.

The facts of Louis Napoleon's rule, as of that of his uncle, belied most of these promises. After the defeat of 1870, the democratic possibility within the nationalist or authoritarian tradition seldom appeared in a consciously Bonapartist form. Indeed, its twentieth-century manifestations have been so varied that the historians in general have not seen fit to juxtapose them. Yet surely one can find a common denominator in such tendencies as the following: the mentality on the eve of the First World War of so many of the youth of France, who followed Charles Péguy in a common cult of the people, the Republic, the Army, and the grandeur of tradition; the rule of the "Jacobin" Clemenceau in the final year of the conflict and his abortive postwar project of a strong presidency; finally, the military aspects of the resistance itself, with its combination of republican loyalty and devotion to the person of an unquestioned chief.

All this is simply to say that de Gaulle and his immediate advisors have not been insincere when they have maintained that the sort of personal rule under which France now lives can be reconciled with democracy and the Republic. In making such a claim, they have a long, if rather spotty, tradition behind them. Indeed, it is the only ideological tradition that has survived reasonably intact the calamities of the past twenty-five years. But this is merely the rhetorical surface of the game. The basic issues lie elsewhere—in the emergence of new forces that are trying to mold the Gaullist regime in the image of their own desires. Ultimately, it will be on the General's ability to assimilate these forces—while still remaining true to his own ideological inspiration—that the historians of the future will judge him.

After the passage of four years, the gloomier predictions of de Gaulle's detractors have not materialized. Indeed, the record, while not exactly the succession of unbroken triumphs that enthusiasts claim, has some rather surprising achievements to show on the credit side. De Gaulle has not only liberated French Africa south of the Sahara; he has begun to resolve the apparently insoluble dilemma of Algeria. Abroad, he has enhanced his country's international standing. At home, at the crest of his authority—the year 1959—he reconciled discordant spirits and gave the French their first experience of civic tranquillity since the late 1920's. And this with less than the anticipated sacrifice of personal freedom. Something beyond a consular "margin" of liberty remains in France today. Censorship of the press and administrative arbitrariness are scarcely more in evidence than they were in the declining days of the Fourth Republic. In the essentials, the French have remained a free people.

Yet that is only part—and perhaps not even the most important part—of the record of the past four years. The France over which de Gaulle presides is a political and ideological vacuum. One reason why he has not become a true dictator is that it has not been necessary for him to do so. There have been no popularly based threats to his authority. On the contrary, the only serious challenges—the uprisings of January, 1960, and April, 1961, in Algiers—have come from despairing military men and North African settlers conscious of the steady ebbing of their support at home. In both cases, the vast majority of Frenchmen—left, right, and center—have closed ranks behind de Gaulle in repressing the insurgents. Thus the result of these abortive military coups has been paradoxical in the extreme. More immediately, it has been to preserve the Republic and democracy against the "fascist" threat. Less obviously, it has further weakened France's democratic institutions by leaving de Gaulle still more alone as his country's sole recourse.

In this situation, both the traditional right and the traditional left have lost their *raison d'être*. The decay of the former is apparent in the erosion of France's multifarious bastions of economic and psychological backwardness—of which the collapse of the Algerian settlers' veto over policy in Paris is merely the most dramatic example. The democratic left puts up a better verbal show—it has with it the major part of the country's articulate intellectuals—but its numbers are small and its accomplishments almost nil. The Algerian war provided its one appealing moral issue and its single notable achievement: by creating a "Dreyfus Case mentality" in Paris in the early autumn of 1960, the left intellectuals played an influential part in pushing de Gaulle toward negotiation with the Moslem rebels.

Since the disappearance of this issue, the democratic left has been stranded without a cause. The more honest of its leaders admit it. They recognize that their position has not substantially changed since the fevered small hours of June 1, 1958, when they registered a *pro forma* vote of no confidence in de Gaulle. Today, as then, they know that there is no practicable alternative; their opposition can do little more than to defend the personal dignity of the intellectual class and the hallowed forms of free speech. The left democrats recognize that they would have no idea how to behave if power should suddenly fall into their hands; de Gaulle knows that there is not the slightest danger of that happening so long as he himself remains capable of rule. Thus there exists a tacit understanding between them which is profoundly demoralizing to the democrats of the left. About the latters' activities there hovers the uneasy doubt that the master of the French is treating them in his customarily patronizing manner as a "kept" opposition. It is significant that in the one case of a serious clash between the two—the "Manifesto of the 121" urging insubordination in the Algerian war—the government soon withdrew the drastic sanctions that in its first flush of anger it had imposed on the signers.

In the meantime, both politics and civic spirit atrophy. De Gaulle and his colleagues "have felt it necessary to seek unity by avoiding debate, by concealing their intentions, and by trying to remove major issues from politics altogether." [1] They govern through sibylline formulas and exhortations. The General has a profound belief in the magic of words (of which he is

1. Philip M. Williams and Martin Harrison, *De Gaulle's Republic* (London: Longmans, 1960), p. 216.

unquestionably a master) and he has stamped the same verbal, rhetorical imprint on his whole regime.[2] But noble phrases can only temporarily plaster over unbridgeable cleavages; in the end even the most prestigious of chiefs is obliged to make a choice, as de Gaulle himself discovered in the case of Algeria.

So the General continues to govern from his lofty height, out of touch with the day-to-day realities of politics and administration, which he leaves to his subordinates. Perhaps he is right in scorning these sordid matters; most of his people show little interest in them either. Yet the result has been to turn the Fifth Republic—whose carefully contrived institutions few seem to take seriously—into something anticipated by neither its creators nor its original critics. It has become a curious reincarnation of a monarchy of the Old Regime. De Gaulle presides over it as the "arbiter" of his people's petty disputes. He has made it evident that he means quite literally the restricted definition of his presidential functions which has long been one of the staples of his public utterances; that is a further reason why his rule has not evolved into a true dictatorship.

Here also there are dangers. In the invertebrate France of today, the rhetoric of official discourse goes along one track, the reality of economic and social evolution follows another. The one group of Frenchmen capable of effective action consists of the modernizers—the enlightened businessmen and civil servants. These people want to develop the tendencies that are already pushing French society and the French econ-

2. See Pierre Viansson-Ponté, "La République du silence," *Le Monde* (Sélection hebdomadaire), XIII (April 28-May 4, 1960), 3.

omy toward the model of its more "advanced" neighbors and allies—Germany, Belgium, Britain, and the
United States. They want to expand industrial production, to rationalize the agrarian economy, and to reduce
the enormously swollen apparatus of distribution. Once
people of this sort followed the lead of Mendès-France;
now they look to de Gaulle. For they know that only a
strong and efficient executive can hope to combat
the entrenched economic interests that used to have a
stranglehold on French parliaments. Their mentality
is "technocratic" and "neocapitalist"; it is by no means
necessarily authoritarian. But under present conditions,
they, like so many other Frenchmen, see no alternative
to the personal rule of de Gaulle.

Obviously the ultimate future belongs to this group.
And in the far future also the structure of French life
will almost necessarily be democratic. The very tendencies which these people are trying to accelerate imply
a democracy of the homogeneous and conformist type
that we have come to associate with advanced industrial nations. It is difficult to think of the eventual solution for France in any other fashion. But in the short
term, the modernizers have to move with caution. Although they are numerous among the French elite,
their electoral base is narrow. The current paralysis on
the left—both Communist and Socialist—has frozen
in place the constituency from which they might otherwise be able to draw recruits. Moreover, their attitude
toward foreign affairs is in conflict with de Gaulle's
most cherished beliefs. By implication, if not always in
conscious theory, the modernizers think in terms of a
"little France" wholly absorbed in the task of its own
self-improvement.

This brings us back to the two de Gaulles with which

we started—de Gaulle the exponent of archaic grandeur, de Gaulle the twentieth-century man. Similarly,
it raises anew the question whether nostalgia for a
glorious past can be reconciled with the technical modernization of French society and the French economy.
Many of the modernizers do not think so. And the
course of recent history seems to be proving them right.
Despite the General's initial assurances to the contrary,
the logic of events has worked toward a concentration
of French efforts on economic expansion and welfare
at home. The talk of an imperial mission that was so
much in evidence at the regime's beginning has become
muted; with dignity, it is true, but more rapidly than
anyone had imagined, de Gaulle has withdrawn step
by step from nearly every French position in Africa.

Eleven years ago—when the Gaullist Rally of the
French People was already falling into difficulties—I
observed that the "ultimate irony" of the General's
intervention in French parliamentary politics had been
that it had revived the old Radicals, the "most unheroic"
of his country's parties.[3] Today a similar irony looms
on the horizon. When Gaullism has become a thing of
the past—when its failures and achievements have
been properly catalogued in the capacious storeroom
of France's ideological heritage—its chief claim to the
gratitude of posterity may simply be that it served as a
temporary vehicle for the "sophisticated conservatism"
of the country's economic modernizers.

Yet the French apparently feel the need of one last
flight into illusion before settling down, as the Germans

3. "Gaullism: Retrospect and Prospect," *Modern France:
Problems of the Third and Fourth Republics,* edited by Edward
Mead Earle (Princeton, N.J.: Princeton University Press, 1951),
p. 263.

and Italians have already done, to the workaday task of taking their normal place in an industrial world. Germany and Italy also went through their period of illusion—and we call it fascism. In France the phase of transition and adjustment is proving less oppressive. It is only by regarding the Gaullist experiment in the light of a long-term adaptation of this sort that we can reconcile its contrasts—its combination of archaism and modernity, of grandiose dreams and sober economic progress.

Here a Bonapartist parallel may once more be helpful. But in this case the comparison extends beyond the personal character of the ruler. "It is not the man who is Bonapartist, it is the situation." [4] In social and economic terms, the situation of France in the 1960's closely resembles what it was exactly a century before.

The period from about 1850 to 1870 was also one of rapid expansion and transformation—the only previous era of French history which brought changes comparable to those the country has been experiencing since the mid 1950's. In the third quarter of the last century, the old framework of French society and politics was cracking: new men and new social classes were emerging into prominence. The local "notables" were losing their grip; the interlocking directorate of enterprising nobles and the conservative upper middle class was no longer running the state and the economy with its former self-assurance. Ever since the Revolution of 1830, it had been apparent that the smaller and middle bourgeoisie were pressing for a share in power. The subsequent Revolution of 1848 proved that this group was not yet equipped to take over; its numbers were

4. Stanley Hoffmann, "Observations sur la crise politique française," *Archives européennes de sociologie*, I (1960), 312.

still too small and it lacked political experience. Three decades were to pass before these new business and professional men were prepared to assume power and to consolidate the institutions of the Third Republic. In the meantime, there yawned a void. The old elite had failed; the new elite was not yet ready. The ambiguous, amorphous regime of Napoleon III filled the gap.

Similarly, today it is apparent that a long-term failure of men and institutions has been the central point of France's contemporary history. No thoughtful Frenchman wants his country to return to the situation of the Third and Fourth Republics. Nearly everyone agrees that the parliamentary regime established in the 1870's proved itself incapable of dealing with the problems of the twentieth century. Its leading representatives—most characteristically, small-town lawyers—demonstrated their incapacity by mishandling or simply shirking the economic issues of the interwar years and the challenge of Nazi Germany. The defeat of 1940 provided one opportunity for renovation—an abortive opportunity, since the circumstances of German occupation nullified whatever drive for genuine reform existed within the Vichy administration. The liberation of 1944 gave France a second chance. This time de Gaulle was in power, and he had a solution prepared, but his country's leading citizens refused to follow him. Fourteen years later, the General had his way. The Fourth Republic had proved to be little more than a feebler version of the Third, and the majority of the French at length drew the conclusion that something more dynamic was required.

So today, like Napoleon III a century earlier, de Gaulle is presiding over a transition to a new type of society that has not yet found its institutional expression. As in the 1860's, the regime finds its support among the vast mass of the inarticulate and the politically unorganized—and rather in the countryside than in the cities—while the more prominent figures of both the left and the right are increasingly disaffected. And just as a hundred years ago, the outlines of the future remain unclear. I defy anyone to forecast the exact shape of French democracy a generation from now. Yet there is an important difference between de Gaulle's position and that of his Bonapartist precursor. While the second of France's emperors imagined that he was establishing a permanent regime, I do not believe the present ruler of the French cherishes any such illusions. He is an elderly man—no longer a prey to vulgar personal ambition—and he prefers the appeasement of civil conflicts to the exercise of arbitrary power. He has no dynasty to found. He resembles the two Napoleons chiefly in the care he has taken to perpetuate his legend—a concern that will doubtless be better served by his now-classic memoirs than the Napoleonic legend was by anything either of the Bonapartes committed to paper. Thus de Gaulle functions, as one moderate oppositionist has put it, as a "great citizen" holding his country's institutions in suspension until the French are once again ready to take charge of their own destinies.

Where does this leave the idea of national "grandeur"? How will such a notion impress the manager-technicians, the highly trained professional people, and the skilled workers, who seem to be emerging as France's new elite? I do not think it will have much appeal for them. *Their* eyes will rather be directed toward efficiency and wider markets and a more rational organization of the continent on which they live. Now that the mirage of a French mission in Africa has vanished, it will be the idea of a united Europe that will fire the imaginations of the young and the daring. The unification of the Western Continent—whether with the six nations alone or on a broader basis—offers the logical target for French ambitions in the new generation. Here practicality and lofty ideals can meet in a fresh interpretation of "grandeur" extending beyond a narrowly nationalist horizon.

This would be de Gaulle's most astounding achievement. If he should put himself in the forefront of the movement for Western European unity and neutrality, he would have attached to his person the deepest mass emotion now in evidence on the European Continent. To do so, he would have to renounce the atomic bomb whose fabrication and testing rank as his greatest error and a crime against humanity. In broader terms, he would have to give up his proud insistence on his country's right to an individual voice in the councils of the great powers. Otherwise the growing band of European neutralists—who already distrust him as a quasi-authoritarian—would never accept his international leadership. To envision de Gaulle as the hope of European neutralism is a paradox that staggers the imagination. But the General has always had a sure sense for mass emotion, and nearly as strange turns of fortune have already occurred in the life of a man who has never let his aims be fettered by petty prejudices and conventions. I for one am not convinced that de Gaulle has yet closed the epic of his own and his country's ideological adventures.

III

THE
RESPONSIBILITY
OF THE
INTELLECTUAL

CHAPTER 10

Is the Intellectual Obsolete?

AN ACQUAINTANCE of mine who knows the Soviet Union well is fond of declaring that in the mid-twentieth century the intellectual has become an anachronism. In the world of advanced industrial society, he argues, the freely speculating mind has lost its function. While I do not agree unreservedly with my pessimistic friend, whose cast of thought leans toward paradox and exaggeration, I am no more willing to reject his argument out of hand. It deserves serious consideration, particularly in our own country, where the present uneasiness of intellectuals strongly suggests that their expectations no longer conform with reality.

We scarcely need to argue the intellectuals' dependence on state and party in the Communist world. These writers and thinkers themselves periodically reveal the facts of the matter by taking advantage of let-ups in official control to voice their long-repressed complaints. Theoretically, organized Marxism has always favored the intellectual estate; and the leaders of contemporary Communism have followed in the established tradition by combatting the normal anti-intellectualism of workingmen and arguing for the ideological solidarity of "workers of brain and hand." Yet the phrase itself betrays the true intention. The brain workers are to share in the construction of socialist society: like the men on the assembly line, they are to make their proper contribution to the new and better world. In brief, their efforts find official favor only—to use an expression that has a familiar American ring—if they are "constructive."

Hence, my friend argues, those whom the Communists call intellectuals are not intellectuals at all in the traditional Western sense. They are no more than "mental technicians." Of course, certain true intellectuals have always existed in the Soviet Union and Eastern Europe—such theoreticians as Varga and Lukács, to whom the authorities have granted a special license. But these are figures of an older generation, whose minds were formed in a very different society. Since the death of Stalin and the relaxation of official pressure that followed it, the younger men have had to start all over again to discover the nature and value of free inquiry.[1]

The small minority of true Communist intellectuals in Eastern Europe still speak a common language with their opposite numbers in the West. And the leading Communist intellectuals of Western Europe for the most part maintain relations with non-Communists of similar caliber. These latter in turn have been in regular communication with their fellows in the United States. In some sense, even in the period of greatest hostility in Soviet-American relations, the chain of international intellectual exchange was never broken. And, after the renewal of Russian contact with the outside world, it was at meetings in Western Europe

1. David Burg, "Observations on Soviet University Students," *The Russian Intelligentsia*, edited by Richard Pipes (New York: Columbia University Press, 1961), pp. 80-100.

that American and Soviet intellectuals first confronted each other in the flesh.

In terms of the contemporary realities of intellectual life, Western Europe offers the logical meeting ground. For it is there that the traditional definition of the intellectual's calling has been most punctiliously adhered to. In Britain, in West Germany, in Italy, and more particularly in France, the status of the thinker or writer as an individual enjoying a special set of privileges and a special kind of respect is very nearly the same as it was two generations ago, on the eve of the great catastrophes that have so profoundly shaken European society. Since then the material circumstances of life have changed vastly—but the central role of the intellectual has remained unimpaired.

At the same time, I suspect that more has actually altered than has appeared on the surface. The European intellectuals continue to write and speak with the old abundance, and their personal doings make as good news copy as in the past. But they no longer have the same practical effect. Today a writers' manifesto could not possibly precipitate a government crisis or start a revolution.[2] Similarly, the efforts of intellectuals to launch new political movements have proved uniformly unsuccessful. From these failures the more honest and perceptive of European writers have begun to draw the deduction that they may be throwing their words into a void—that the old exchange between the intellectual and his public is turning into a weary and repetitious monologue. Few of them are thinking of aban-

2. Even the 1960 "Manifesto of the 121," as I suggested in Chapter 9, was symptomatic less of the intellectuals' power than of their reduced circumstances in Gaullist France.

doning their calling; but a great many are searching for a redefinition of it that may give it greater contemporary relevance.

The apathy and lack of understanding for things intellectual of which American writers complain may very well, then, be a contemporary phenomenon extending far beyond the confines of the United States. The situation in our country may mark a halfway point between the declared hostility to free speculation characteristic of the Soviet Union and the traditional (and increasingly hollow) respect that the public in Western Europe accords. Moreover, there is a genuineness in the American attitude that makes it easier to examine: where inherited ritual does not require that people pretend to a higher regard for the things of the mind than they actually feel, the realities emerge more sharply. In this perspective, the intellectual situation of the United States offers a paradigm for the whole of industrial society in the twentieth century.

Initially it is well to remind ourselves of those aspects of the American intellectual heritage that have set it off from the European. Here I think we can safely accept my friend's distinction between "mental technicians" and true intellectuals. A distinction of this sort has been implicit in the attitude of Europeans since the role of the free intellectuals first differentiated itself from that of the clergy. When in early modern times the lay thinker and writer began to break the original Church monopoly of intellectual life, he inherited most of the respect and sense of differentiated function that adhered to the priestly status. Although no longer bound by holy orders, he remained a "clerk" in spirit and function. Hence Julien Benda was holding true to tradition when a generation ago he rebuked the modern "clerks" for a betrayal of their historic mission.[3]

Yet not all those of mental training inherited this benefit of clergy. The sense of differentiated status did not apply to physicians, engineers, or technical advisers to government. Only those who performed the *same sort* of functions that the clergy had once monopolized —and, in a more restricted area, continued to perform —enjoyed the latters' special immunity. Only those engaged in abstract speculation, in the posing of general problems of universal concern, were able to make a valid claim to a privileged status.

Moreover, as opposed to technical pursuits on the one hand and to merely personal investigations on the other, the function of the new and the old "clerks" in Europe always bore a *public* character. The respect these individuals enjoyed did not derive simply from the splendor of their mental operations; it reflected their position as the custodians of the higher values of society. As the Church had once enunciated the general principles that were to guide public conduct, as the clerically dominated universities had elaborated the rules of argumentation and served as the guardians of orthodoxy, so from the sixteenth century on the new class of lay intellectuals began to elaborate a richer and less confined pattern of behavior for their fellow citizens. When Erasmus or Bacon wrote, he did not write for a narrow coterie of intellectuals; he spoke to the princes and governing elite of Europe.

It was only by a series of slow and cautious adaptations that this definition of public responsibility began

3. *La Trahison des clercs* (Paris: Bernard Grasset, 1927), translated as *The Betrayal of the Intellectuals* (Boston: Beacon Press paperback, 1955).

to be widened into a concept of the liberty of the intellectual to speculate without restraint on the frontiers
of knowledge. The modern idea of the freedom of the
mind certainly does not much antedate Milton—and
even Milton showed no tolerance toward Papists and
atheists. Indeed, it is doubtful whether such an idea
could ever have won its way at all if those who advanced it had not been surrounded by some of the sanc-
tified respect derived from their clerical origin, and,
concomitantly, if it had not been implied that the
claimants to intellectual freedom would always be few
in number.

So by the eighteenth century there had come about
the radical change that converted the characteristic European intellectual from a defender and rationalizer of
existing institutions into their implacable critic. This
latter role is so familiar to us today that we seldom
stop to recall how it marked a nearly complete reversal
of the older function. Throughout the century and a
half immediately preceding our own era, it was generally assumed that the most alert and active section of
the intelligentsia would "nibble at the foundations of
. . . society." [4] And that is what an old-type European
intellectual such as Jean-Paul Sartre still thinks he is
about.

Never in its history—except perhaps in the 1930's
and early 1940's—did the United States conform to
this European model. Starting from a similar clerical
monopoly of intellectual leadership, the American colonies never developed a true intellectual caste. When
the domination of Protestant divines was shaken off, no

4. Joseph A. Schumpeter, *Capitalism, Socialism, and Democracy*, Third Edition (New York: Harper & Brothers, 1950), p.
151.

native-grown intelligentsia stepped into their place. In the early days of the Republic, the life of the mind was still inextricably entangled with statesmanship; we have only to think of Franklin and Jefferson and John Quincy Adams. Later there appeared the sages of Concord and the wits of Manhattan—but they did not form a homogeneous class exerting a cumulative influence on a national scale. Until the twentieth century, the educated American might be a statesman or a preacher, a *littérateur* or a technician, but only a handful of isolated figures such as Henry Adams behaved like intellectuals in the European sense.

It was Henry Adams who in the 1870's trained some of the first American Ph.D.'s. The creation of a substantial group of individuals with doctor's degrees brought the United States closer to European conditions; the man endowed with an academic doctorate—and usually with a job he considered unworthy of his talents—had become a typical figure among the Continental intelligentsia. Simultaneously the American institutions of higher learning began to convert themselves into universities in the European sense; professors ceased to be mere pedagogues and sought to supplement their teaching with independent thought and investigation. Yet in the population at large the older attitude persisted; the characteristic young man of brains and promise became a "mental technician" rather than an intellectual. It is symptomatic that even today the physician ranks higher than the professor or writer in the scale of public prestige.

Hence the substantial influence that American intellectuals enjoyed in the period from 1933 to 1945 was something unprecedented in our history. And it is not surprising that it proved rather heady to modest professors who suddenly found themselves pulled out of quiet campuses into the bustle and excitement of Washington. What is less understandable is the fashion in which many of them began to take their new situation for granted and to treat it as their due. In this case, the wisdom of Napoleon's mother—"pourvou que ça doure"—would have been a more sensible attitude. Once the extraordinary conditions of depression and war were over—and once a corps of technical career administrators had been trained to fill the gaps in the service for which it had been necessary to improvise talent from the outside—the more normal American attitude toward direction by intellectuals quite predictably resumed its sway.

In judging the anti-intellectualism of the last decade and a half, it is important to separate what has been truly new and threatening from what has been merely the reassertion of an earlier and more usual attitude. Certainly part of the American intellectual's sense of precarious status has stemmed from an exaggerated notion of what that status had actually become. It was not true—as both the critics and the defenders of the intellectuals frequently seemed to assert—that in the 1930's and 1940's a group of doctrinaire thinkers and professors had held the destiny of the country in their hands. Nor was it true that any but a tiny minority of them had consciously sought positions of influence. Rather, they had accepted, often with reluctance, duties that their country had urged upon them. And these they had accomplished with conscientiousness, if necessarily in somewhat amateurish fashion. When the crisis—or rather, the series of crises—was over, they were dropped from the service, or, more usually, they left of their own accord, drawn away by nostalgia for

the campus and the sense that there was no longer in-
teresting or useful work in Washington to be performed.

Thus when American intellectuals voice their grievances—and I would be the last to deny that many of
these grievances are very real—they had better omit the
charge of ingratitude on the part of their government.
They would do well to combat in themselves the hurt
feelings that have produced the two equally undignified
attitudes of recrimination and self-flagellating apology
for past errors of judgment. It would be far better for
them to remember that they were neither obliged nor
entitled by right to work for the government: they chose
of their own free will to serve the state, and in so doing
they took certain inevitable risks. They stuck their
heads into the lion's den and it was only to be expected that now and then the lion would bite.

Finally, American intellectuals would do well to recall that in their government service they did not function *as intellectuals* but as "mental technicians." They
had assigned jobs to do; they were not free to speculate as their fancy directed. Or, if they did choose to
speculate in academic fashion, they ran the danger of
going astray and of saying or doing something that in
retrospect would look rather foolish. By serving their
country they lost some of their independence: *as intellectuals,* their position was diminished rather than
enhanced. And the same is true of those who more
recently have accepted the favors of government or of
business. The intellectuals who in the years after 1945
retired from public service and returned to teaching or
writing displayed a surer sense of where their own
peculiar values could best be cultivated. Without his
freedom to speculate at will, they saw, the intellectual
could function only haltingly.

*   *   *

In the period from the presidential election of 1952 to the congressional election of 1954, the American intellectuals closed their ranks and manifested an unprecedented corporate solidarity. For the first time in recent history, the intellectual leadership of the country in its overwhelming majority backed a single political party. Earlier, in the depression and war years, American writers and professors had divided along the usual political cleavages: while the most vocal and active of their number had supported the New Deal, a relatively quiet minority had remained Republican, and a smaller although more advertised minority had espoused Communism or near-Communism. By 1952, both left and right had disappeared. Overnight nearly everyone had become a Stevenson Democrat.

The unity of the years 1952 to 1954 showed a clear awareness of a very real danger. It suggested that American intellectuals had at last come of age and knew how to go about defending the values that gave their lives meaning. They had correctly sensed that the agitation directed by Senator McCarthy and his like struck at the whole notion of free inquiry and that supporting the Democratic party was the most realistic way to hit back. For it was apparent that the Republican leadership was "soft," to say the least, toward the enemies of intellectual values, and that if elected to office it would give no reliable protection to the personal security of the writer or scholar.

The conduct of the Eisenhower administration during the first part of its tenure proved this assumption correct. And the changes that occurred after 1954 came about independently or even against the will of the administration.[5] The Republicans notably extended the range of arbitrary security procedures until they were brought up short, not by a spontaneous attack of conscience, but by a series of peremptory orders from the federal courts. Except in the vague sense of exuding a spirit of fairness and eliminating the main pretext for civic bitterness by bringing the Korean war to an end, President Eisenhower can not be held responsible for the freer intellectual atmosphere of the past eight years.

What has actually occurred has been far less dramatic than the self-congratulations of Americans would lead us to believe. The personalization of the threat to intellectual freedom under the name of "McCarthyism" obscured its true nature and extent. Senator McCarthy was only the most spectacular and extreme representative of a way of thinking that in some form or other gripped the greater part of the American citizenry. His political collapse did not end the agitation for limiting freedom of thought; it merely institutionalized it and made it respectable. The subsequent improvement in the civic atmosphere has concealed the permanent fashion in which that atmosphere has deteriorated during the past seventeen years. We are living at a higher level of freedom than a decade ago—but this level is perceptibly below that to which we were accustomed before 1945. We have learned to take for granted official and semi-official procedures—a whole ramifying network of "clearances," denunciations, and nearly invisible taboos—that are novelties in the American constitutional tradition. Indeed, questions of personal freedom have passed outside the sphere of parti-

5. See Chapter 11.

san debate. In the last two presidential campaigns, the two parties have substantially agreed that the post-McCarthy combination of allowing the more notorious administrative innovations to lapse, and regularizing those that remain, is precisely what the country requires.

In short, the situation has settled down to what can be considered "normal" for the postwar period; there are even signs that with the almost uninterrupted series of international crises over the past year, a new wave of McCarthyism is on the way. Under these circumstances, it is incumbent on American writers and scholars to rethink their relationship to their fellow citizens and to the state—that whole "public" aspect of their endeavors that has never been absent from the Western intellectual tradition.

In this re-evaluation, the American intellectuals should first of all consider the question of their own threatened obsolescence. In a highly developed industrial society such as ours, to pose the problem of whether the freely speculating mind has lost its function is more than paradox-mongering. The range of such speculation has certainly been reduced; what part public pressure has played in this process, and what part is due to a failure of mental initiative, is far from clear. In any case, it is apparent that a number of questions that used to be hotly debated have ceased to agitate any large number of people. We are living in a society and in an era where there is scope for relatively few intellectuals. Supply is outrunning demand: the colleges and graduate schools are turning out an ever-increasing quantity of degree holders who fancy themselves dedicated to free speculation, but who in fact can find no employment worthy of their talents.

Nor is the academic job market taking care of the matter as tidily as one might presume. Today—as opposed to ten years back—positions are available for all the Ph.D.'s that the universities are currently producing or are likely to produce. Within another decade there will be a real shortage of intellectually trained personnel. But these present and future vacancies will not call for *intellectuals*: they will require "mental technicians"—experts for the business world, civil servants, and, above all, pedagogues to teach routine courses. Such jobs will not be what their incumbents originally aimed at; the genuine intellectual outlets will be scarcely more numerous than before.

These future intellectuals *manqués* can at least find comfort in the reflection that they will be filling an urgent national need. The true writers and scholars, on the contrary, may increasingly question the usefulness of their own traditional pursuits. They are likely to be troubled in particular by doubts as to the present-day relevance of their eighteenth- and nineteenth-century role as society's mentors and critics.

Today in America most people either pretend to esteem, or actually think they do esteem, an institution or an ideal that is not what they imagine it to be. The objects that are customarily held up to our reverence are respectable enough in themselves. But they have become so shopworn in the course of systematic manipulation to practical ends, so twisted in the service of propagandist aims, that they have lost their original flavor and their connection with the reality of human experience out of which they grew. They have been so tossed about from hand to hand, so rubbed and soiled by use, that they have become all mixed up—the names blurred or distorted or simply assigned to new objects bearing practically no relation to those originally thus labeled. And so there has fallen to our intellectuals a task of social criticism of a new type, a vast job of unscrambling disfigured concepts and re-establishing them in their proper usages. It is the twentieth-century variant of the old task of calling things by their right names—a function that derives from Socrates.

Socrates we think of primarily as a great teacher. And since everyone who writes is a teacher—whether or not he has any formal academic connection—the problem of Socrates' career has always held a passionate interest for writers and intellectuals in general. We think of him as a seeker after truth; the Athenian government condemned him as a corrupter of the young. Actually, the two functions were inseparable. Socrates, like any good teacher, could pursue truth only at the risk of corruption. He could not seek out the essence of wisdom and justice without baring his skepticism about the workings of Athenian democracy. And the Athenian authorities, in presenting him the hemlock, were only asserting the same right—in rather more drastic form—that so many American public and university administrations arrogated to themselves during the McCarthy era.

The problem of who behaved correctly—Socrates or his judges—is insoluble in any absolute sense. The right of the intellectual to speak his mind and the right of the organized community to defend itself against potential subversion are both honored principles. But for the intellectual himself there can be only one answer. The sort of self-consorship that is going on today —the widespread reluctance to raise one's voice in a period of emergency—betrays a serious confusion of ideas. It is not up to the intellectual himself to decide where his quest for truth should stop; that is the function of the public authorities. If he is true to his calling, a teacher will follow his thought wherever it may lead him. Perhaps he will exercise some care in choosing the forum for expressing it: in an age of intellectual simplification, the chances are legion that someone will misunderstand his ideas—or wilfully distort them to partisan ends. And he may always decide to maintain a prudent silence when it becomes obvious that the next step will bring on the hemlock. These, however, are purely personal considerations—reminders that the intellectual is also a human being, with ties to normal living and a family which he must protect from want and humiliation. *As* intellectual, he has only the code of the truth as he sees it.

Necessarily, then, the American intellectual of today finds himself both a teacher and a corrupter of youth. The two functions, I think, have always been inseparable. But in the past three-quarters of a century it has been peculiarly apparent that the true teachers, the true creators of the twentieth-century mind, have been great destroyers. We may think of Nietzsche—the first and perhaps the most influential of the corrupters—and then of such men as Freud and Gide. All these writers worried mightily over the effects of their teachings; they quite rightly feared the process of vulgarization and sensationalizing that would distort their most precious ideas almost beyond recognition. Just before his death, Gide was appalled at the statement of a juvenile assassin that no one who had not read the writings of the great "immoralist" could possibly understand his crime. Like Nietzsche, Gide maintained his Protestant conscience to the end. He could only pray that his disciples would learn from him—and then do otherwise.

In cases such as these, Goethe's injunction to youthful admirers of his *Werther*—"be a man and do not follow me"—epitomizes the intellectual's divided mind. In a period when even abstract criticism may prove politically inexpedient, the teacher must lead a kind of double life. He may not foreswear his function of critic—but he may warn his students of the perils in following the implications of his thought to their extreme conclusions. He may express to them his grave doubts as to the future, he may subject to the most searching scrutiny the manners and institutions of his countrymen—and then suggest that the role of nonconformist will suit only a small minority of them. This attitude on the part of the teacher is neither hypocritical nor evasive. It is simply the way a conscientious man has to behave in trying to reconcile his responsibilities as a seeker after truth with a scrupulous performance of his duties as a citizen. Such an attitude is relatively new to Americans. But in the rest of the world it is as old as organized society. Particularly in times of clerical domination—which the present orthodoxy of Americanism recalls—the double standard of the intellectual and the citizen has been the only recourse for the sensitive thinker intent on maintaining his integrity in two distinct realms.

Indeed, the realms of thought and of practical living *are* distinct. And much of the confusion, lack of poise, and self-abasement of the American intellectual springs from his failure to recognize this difference. He tries to behave—to speak, to entertain himself, to drink—like his fellow citizens; and then he wonders why this course leaves him unhappy and disoriented. Lacking pride in his distinctness, is he justified in complaining that the rest of his countrymen do not rate him sufficiently highly?

The American intellectual needs to have more pride. He needs to assert with more intransigence his own standards and the characteristics that mark him off from his neighbors. And, in particular, he needs to emphasize that, in an era of conformism, it is his function to maintain the principle of nonconformity. Outwardly, he may behave as others do: within, he stands alone. All too often, the price of this attitude will be an increasing loneliness. But anyone who is not prepared to undergo loneliness should never have chosen to be an intellectual. Anyone who is not willing to face the implications of his own thought—to see the present in all its baffling and disturbing complexity—is not worthy of his calling. The "terrible simplifiers" are already with us. They do not yet rule our nation—but they have begun to extend their rule over our minds. The American writer and teacher alone can offer a serious resistance to the floodtide of intellectual cheapness, distortion, and half-thought. And, in so doing, he will perform an act of negation so strong and passionate as to become an affirmation—the affirmation of love for what is clear and fair and honest. What wonder if in the process he runs the risk of being called a corrupter?

All this suggests that in the years to come the American intellectual is likely to find his calling increasingly incompatible with service to government or business—except, perhaps, for temporary arrangements of an episodic or crisis character. Indeed, the first weeks of

the Kennedy administration brought tragic proof of
what happens when writers and scholars are subjected
to the pressures of such conflicting loyalties. The landing in Cuba severely tried the consciences of the intellectuals whom the new President had called to Washington. No doubt it revolted the great majority of them.
But none resigned. Their sense of duty to the state
proved stronger than individual moral scruple.

Such is the eventual choice that faces the writer or
scholar in government. In the final reckoning, he is
obliged to decide between resignation from public
service or the sacrifice of his personal ethic to reason
of state. Under these circumstances, I think, most intellectuals will refrain from the temptations of office.
At the same time, they need not feel totally isolated.
The beginnings of corporative solidarity among American writers and scholars that became evident during
the early 1950's have outlasted the period of maximum
pressure against them. And this is quite as it should be.
In an era in which labor, business, and other groups
of citizens bound together by common interests are accustomed to make known their wants to government
and the public through some kind of corporative organization, the intellectuals are gradually coming to
realize that they, too, need to be similarly equipped.
Such groupings as the American Association of University Professors, the Civil Liberties Union, and the numerous *ad hoc* pools of financial resources that have
seen threatened individuals through a series of victo-
rious court battles have become permanent and necessary features of the American intellectual scene.

Yet the newly found corporate solidarity among
American intellectuals will prove of no avail unless the
group in question is narrowly and rigorously delimited.

ficult to find excuses for the conduct of a man who bore the marks of respectability and who represented one of the best-educated constituencies in the country.

It is only when one talks to the very young that one realizes how devastating the legacy of the McCarthy years has been. The college generation of today has quite literally had to learn its political and ideological vocabulary from scratch. For the better part of a decade the motto "Don't sign or join anything" recommended itself to ambitious youth; almost no fundamental issue was publicly discussed. Not until 1957 was the post-McCarthy slumber broken with the launching of the first important nonconformist effort— the Committee for a Sane Nuclear Policy. In the meantime, the young people and students accepted as normal the detailed scrutiny of their opinions (and even sexual attitudes) by an army of government sleuths. And we, their professors, mostly submitted to being questioned about our students—choosing the lesser evil, for fear that if we refused to answer, we would jeopardize their chances for public service. Yet this seemed a sorry return for the splendid fashion in which the students themselves had not told on *us* when the going was rough in the period between Eisenhower's inauguration and McCarthy's fall.

The record is not a pretty one. Very few people have anything to be proud of—no more than a distinguished minority of American intellectuals and certainly not the Democratic party. Although Adlai Stevenson made a number of noble statements during the campaign of 1952, and although many of the nonprofessional enthusiasts whom that campaign mobilized into service thought of it as a battle more against McCarthy than

An indiscriminate welcoming of mere hangers-on will do no good and may greatly harm the cause of liberal inquiry. At a time when the whole notion of the freely speculating mind has been called into question and will almost certainly continue under periodic attack, the intellectuals will be able to defend themselves only if they convince their fellow citizens of the responsibility and seriousness of their calling. Dilettantism will not help—nor will the production of bright ideas for practical purposes, masking as intellectual activity. Those undertaking a career as writer or scholar would do well to put themselves some searching questions as to whether they are psychologically equipped to carry out what they intend.

I do not believe that the intellectual—and more particularly the American intellectual—is obsolete. But I do believe he faces a dubious future. He will confront a public only sporadically (and then often dangerously) interested in what he does. He will be obliged to withstand the pressures, massive and subtle alike, that will urge on him the role of a mental technician. Assaulted in *both* of his historic functions—as the ideological bulwark of society and as its utopian critic—he may himself begin to doubt the relevance of his pursuits. His path will be a very special one; it will not be for the half-hearted.

CHAPTER 11

Why We Had No Dreyfus Case

THE "McCarthy era" of American history officially ended with the censure of the Wisconsin Senator by his colleagues in the autumn of 1954. His death two and a half years later only seemed to confirm what the verdict of his fellow Senators had already announced —that the influence he had wielded over American life had vanished even more swiftly and inexplicably than it had appeared. Soon people began to speak in the past tense of the methods which had been associated with his name. The implication was that informing on others—and the subtle but tormenting fears that went along with it—had ceased to be a feature of the American scene. Those citizens (mostly intellectuals) whom revulsion from McCarthy's ways had aroused to militance relaxed their previous sense of urgency. The battle for freedom, they thought, had been triumphantly concluded.

A moment's reflection might have shown them that this was far from true. McCarthy had not succumbed to the righteous indignation of the American intellectual community. He had been condemned by his peers on narrow grounds—for little more than a breach of

senatorial courtesy—and the wider issue of what he stood for had never been settled. President Ei hower and his immediate subordinates never adm that they had done wrong during the year when had tried to "appease" the demagogue from Wisco Secretary of State Dulles continued to wrap himse the garb of a moralist, and the public forgot ho had sacrificed experienced and devoted diploma McCarthy's wrath. It is symptomatic of the extr limited nature of the anti-McCarthy victory that two presidential candidates chosen six years late was thought to have opposed the senatorial reso of censure, while the other had abstained from vot

A few individual injustices were rectified afte Carthy's fall. But there was no wholesale reha tion of the innocent nor punishment of the Where a liberalization of policy occurred—as matter of passports—it was not President Eise himself who acted, but the courts which forced tant administration to correct the abuses that come established as public policy. Only a among the citizenry called for the abolition Carthy's forum, the Senate Internal Security mittee. And after the Democrats gained contr Senate and took over the subcommittee's chair it continued to coerce witnesses into "naming by pressures that were quieter than McCart closely resembled them. The questioning of Li ing in the summer of 1960 was a particularly example of procedures which recalled the gr from 1950 to 1954. While Senator Eastland sissippi was in charge, this might be explai as a regrettable example of backwoods behav Senator Dodd of Connecticut took over, it be

against Eisenhower, the majority of organization Democrats—including, of course, the young paladin who
was to lead them to victory in 1960—treated the whole
issue as merely peripheral and embarrassing.

Here Truman bears a heavy responsibility. No doubt
he was outraged by McCarthy's methods. But he failed
to take the one action that might have cleared the air
and substituted historical fact for murky suspicion. By
his original gesture of dismissing the issue of Communists in government as a "red herring," he tied his
party's hands for an effective defense or counterattack
against such a charge in the years that followed. By
refusing to admit that Communists had in fact "pene-
trated" the federal service during the New Deal and
war years, he made it impossible to discuss honestly in
public the extent of that penetration and how much it
had actually accomplished.

How many Communists succeeded in entering federal service? Estimates vary, but the number cannot
be higher than a few hundred, mostly in the newer war
agencies. How much influence did they exert on policy?
Only three or four possible Communists were ever
identified in positions of high responsibility. Did the
majority of Communists in government profit from their
positions to engage in conspiratorial or treasonous activities? Here the answer is an emphatic no. From my
own experience as a State Department official during a
period when Communists were still in government service, I can vouch for the fact that most of them honestly tried to do the job assigned, with their peculiar
ideology deflecting their judgment only now and then,
but most of the time simply adding a certain zeal and
seriousness to the performance of their duties. When
and how did they leave the federal government? Here

my memories check with the fragmentary official statements emanating from the Truman administration.
Nearly all the Communists resigned during the year
and a half immediately following the war. Most left of
their own volition, having concluded that the atmosphere in Washington was no longer propitious. Others
were eased out, through forced resignations or intima-
tions that their usefulness had come to an end. Some of
the procedures employed in removing them were extremely harsh, and a number of non-Communists also
found themselves obliged to resign; but at least the
thing was done in private, the fiction of resignation
was preserved, and individuals dropped from federal
service did not experience as severe difficulties in finding private employment as were encountered subsequently by those purged in the McCarthy era.

These are the approximate facts. I should add a
summary statement of the conclusions that historians
have reached on the three areas of war and postwar
policy in which Communist influence was supposed to
have been most important—Yalta, China, and Germany.

On Yalta the evidence is conclusive. The publication of the private records of the conference in the mid
1950's proved disappointing to those Republicans who
had hoped to draw political profit from them. Far from
documenting any sort of treason, these papers failed
to show that Alger Hiss (whose case, by the way,
must be regarded as still open) had played an influential role, and further demonstrated that on one of
the few occasions when he was consulted Hiss advised
resistance to Soviet demands. In short, the Yalta docu-
ments contained none of the sensational revelations
that Roosevelt's enemies had promised.

On China, the evidence is more tangled. But from the mass of controversy and recrimination, three central facts emerge. First, the advisors on China policy who were later pilloried and hounded from government service were guilty of nothing worse than an honest error of judgment: they underestimated the Marxist ruthlessness of the Communist leaders. Secondly, these diplomats were not Communists themselves. Third, their advice did not decisively alter the course of events. I know of no qualified expert on China who denies that Mao Tse-tung and his associates would have come to power in any case; the only remote chance of preventing Communist victory lay in a massive American military effort which stood no chance of popular acceptance in the prevailing postwar mood of "get the boys home" as fast as possible.

On German policy alone, I think, some case for Communist influence can be made. My own impression during service as an OSS officer in Germany during the summer and autumn of 1945 was that two or three American Communists with high positions in the economic branches of military government were urging a punitive policy that was consciously intended to favor Soviet aims. But this type of assertion is extremely hard to document. At the close of the war, a punitive attitude toward Germany was by no means restricted to Communists; many American Jews, for example, were understandably anxious to revenge the murder of six million of their coreligionists. Here, as in the China case, pro-Communist attitudes were not decisive in altering American actions. After a few months of confusion, our government settled into a reasonably coherent and constructive policy of rebuilding the German economy and German democratic institutions.

Such is the defense that President Truman might have made of the first year and a half of his administration. He might have stated quite frankly that in the "Popular Front" atmosphere of the decade 1935-1945 some Communists did indeed enter the federal service. He might have added that in the very different ideological climate of the opening phases of the cold war these Communists were quietly eased out—indeed, that virtually all of them had departed *more than two years* before McCarthy blew his opening trumpet with his famous speech detailing the number of "subversives" in the Department of State. The President might have concluded that during their brief stay in Washington the Communists had accomplished very little indeed. Truman said none of these things—or at least said none of them completely and unequivocally. This is one reason why America in the early 1950's never had its Dreyfus Case.

I mean that we did not have our Dreyfus Affair in the sense that there emerged no single test case which could serve as a symbol and a battle cry to all who felt themselves threatened or whom a more abstract indignation had aroused to champion the cause of justice. Unlike France at the turn of the century, the United States in the 1950's did not find the human being whose plight could dramatize the whole issue and whose triumphal acquittal by the courts could serve as a stinging rebuke to the administration and a precedent for rehabilitating all the others who had suffered from the arbitrary acts of public officials.

There were two possible contenders for the role of test case. One, of course, was Alger Hiss, and initially many liberals rallied to his support. But as the evidence presented in Hiss's two trials became increasingly damning, most of those who had at first been ready to spring to his defense concluded that he might well be guilty—or at the very least, that the case was insufficiently clear to serve as a general test. A minority of men of good will stuck with Hiss to the last and have never stopped asserting his innocence. A great many more—and I count myself among them—remained unconvinced of his guilt, or at least of his guilt as charged by Whittaker Chambers. In the case of Captain Dreyfus, the innocence of the accused eventually became clear to everyone not irremediably prejudiced against him. In the case of Alger Hiss, this was far from true. To this day, doubt has persisted: the overwhelming suspicion remains that, for reasons which have still to be explained, both the prosecution and the defense tried to conceal relevant information; the full context of the events in question has never emerged.

The case of Owen Lattimore at first sight appeared more promising. For he had been merely a government consultant rather than a public official like Hiss. (Most liberal-minded people, I think, were willing to grant, as I would, the right of the federal government to protect itself against spies and saboteurs by removing Communists from the truly "sensitive" positions in the foreign and defense establishments.) Moreover, in the case of Lattimore, the charge of Communist affiliation rested on nothing but innuendo; it never came remotely close to being proved. When all the deceptive verbiage of his accusers had been stripped away, the worst that could be said against him was that he had made pro-Soviet statements and given bad advice on China policy.

Surely these were insufficient reasons for pillorying him in public and nearly destroying his position as a scholar. The injustice was patent. Still the American intellectual community held back; only a minority rallied to Lattimore's defense. People found all sorts of reasons for reluctance, besides fear for their own jobs, which was mostly unadmitted. More particularly, they found a lack of total candor in Lattimore's replies to Senator McCarthy. Here they forgot a simple psychological fact: it is hard to keep clear-headed and consistent in facing a bully. Beyond that, most American liberals were seeking the impossible; they were looking for a perfect test case. They forgot—if they ever knew—that Captain Dreyfus had been far from an ideal witness in his own defense and that from the personal standpoint he left much to be desired. In the great imperfection of human affairs, ideal test cases seldom appear. We have to take our issues where we find them. We have to fight our ideological and moral battles, not on ground of our own choosing, but on the foggy and swampy terrain which our enemies have selected.

But this was not all. American liberals and radicals were uneasy in their consciences. They could not spring to the defense of others because they were unsure of their own innocence.

This was McCarthy's greatest triumph. This was the abiding poison he left with us. He succeeded in creating a sense of guilt among thousands of intelligent and public-spirited people—a large part of the intellectual and moral elite of the nation. Not only did he deprive the government of their service and counsel during a decade when these were badly needed. He crippled their own thought by stirring within them the demon of self-doubt. McCarthy and his aides had never made a systematic study of psychoanalytic theory. But their infernal intuition had revealed to them one of its essential discoveries—that it is precisely the most conscientious and scrupulous people who suffer from the heaviest burden of unconscious guilt.

Thus each man who felt even remotely threatened by the wave of "security" discharges and sanctions began to scrutinize his own conscience and to assess exactly how guilty he himself had been. There grew up a cult of fine distinctions and careful gradations of guilt. People forgot that when large moral issues are in play, fine distinctions are useless—or worse than useless. When spiritual and intellectual survival is at stake —as was quite literally true in this country from 1950 to 1954—it is a simple question of "we" against "they." The barricades are up, and we cannot afford to be choosy about those who are fighting beside us. Rather than splitting hairs over whether or not a Communist should be fired from a university teaching post—a common-sense answer was that he should not, since the psychological havoc on the campus which would result from his discharge far outbalanced any presumed gain in protecting the minds of the young—the liberal intellectuals would have done better to close ranks and to proclaim their solidarity with the vast majority of the accused. Nor would they have had to make an explicit exception for the tiny minority of spies and saboteurs whom millions of man-hours of government sleuthing every so often unearthed. For these did not fall into the category of the ideologically persecuted. They came rather under the jurisdiction of the ordinary criminal procedure by which *any* government— even the most tolerant, like that of Great Britain— has traditionally tried to protect itself from harm.

What exactly did liberals find themselves guilty of when they scrutinized their own consciences? "Softness" toward Russia? Illusions about Communist China? A nostalgia for the Soviet-American solidarity which had won the struggle against fascism? A failure to detect the Communist inspiration of their acquaintances who had involved them in fine-sounding "front" activities? That was about all. What it added up to was a rather vague and blundering protest against the dissolution of the antifascist solidarity of wartime and the drift toward the division of the world into two armed camps in the years after 1945.

More concretely, the ideological attitude of many liberals in the later 1940's betrayed two serious weaknesses. It indulged in "wave of the future" reasoning —assuming the eventual victory of Communism without inquiring sufficiently what could be done to deflect its triumphant course, and softening the outlines of Communism itself to make that victory more palatable. It also inclined toward overcompensation. Suspecting that the anti-Communists exaggerated the abuses of Soviet despotism, a large number of generous-minded Americans jumped to the conclusion that the reverse must be true. They found it difficult to believe in the reality of the Russian forced-labor camps. They refused to plumb the depths of evil in Stalin's soul: they had vented the one great hatred of their lives on the person of Hitler, and they could not summon up the same unforgiving wrath against a second tyrant. For tens of thousands of articulate Americans over the age of thirty, the struggle against fascism had been the central moral experience of their youth; they did not have the heart to remobilize their energies for another such combat.

The chief sin of this type of thinking was what came to be called "anti-anti-Communism." To balance its lack of realism, we may recall certain of its other aspects, which seemed utopian at the time but which ten years later have a much more sensible look—a refusal to consider the world as irrevocably split and a concern for keeping open bridges across the great ideological divide, more particularly to those nations (like India) or groups (like European neutralists) which were trying to remain uncommitted in the cold war. Such were the constructive features of the "anti-anti-Communist" position. Along with them went a prophetic understanding of the moral debasement that the anti-Communist crusade would inflict on the American people.

For all their faults, Americans of this variety did far less harm than their adversaries.[1] They also did less harm than the other kind of liberals who aided in the early stages of the anti-Communist drive from 1945 to 1950. After McCarthy himself went into action and pushed the campaign against "subversives" far beyond their original intention, many of the anti-Communist liberals regretted what they had done—as one, I remember, was honest enough to tell me at the high point of the Senator's power in 1953. But by then it was too

1. I scarcely need add that I dissent strenuously from what I regard as a pernicious conclusion by Leslie A. Fiedler ("We liberals . . . have . . . done great evil") in "Hiss, Chambers, and the Age of Innocence," *An End to Innocence* (Boston: Beacon Press paperback, 1955), p. 24.

late. He and his fellow Sorcerer's Apprentices had helped to unleash forces over which they had totally lost control.

A moral debasement—that was the ultimate legacy of the McCarthy era. Or rather, a moral numbness. Most people were not corrupted by what they went through or what they saw going on around them. They were simply stunned by it. Better still, they were confirmed in a habit of mental dissociation and compartmentalized thinking that the conclusion of the war itself had made a psychological necessity.

When the atomic bomb dropped over Hiroshima in August, 1945, I recall sensing that the world had suddenly stood still and that life would never be the same again. I suspect a great many of my countrymen felt the same way. The experience was not exactly one of personal or national guilt. It was that something so awful (in both senses of the term) had happened that the usual criteria for judging men and events would no longer serve. It was an *impersonal* experience—a shock from outside so enormous that the only way one felt able to deal with it was by dissociating oneself and refusing to think about it. More than a decade was to pass before I could bear to concentrate my mind on the question of nuclear warfare.

The shock of Hiroshima confirmed a national tendency which had begun to manifest itself with the terror bombing of German cities in the two years preceding. It marked a further—and perhaps decisive—stage in an erosion of moral responses. Our ruthless obliteration of German dwellings and cultural landmarks, far beyond any clear military necessity, had evoked almost no protest at home; the same lack of moral indignation was apparent half a decade later, when the American public accepted as quite natural the napalm bombing of Korean villages. Those rare individuals who did object usually did so in the privacy of their own consciences. Public protest seemed futile; a pall of dull acceptance settled over the American soul.

It would be tempting to investigate how much this change in attitude had to do with the vogue of a fatalistic neoreligiosity that became apparent at the same time. Certainly the young people who in these years took so kindly to Kierkegaard and Dostoevski found in such authors' bleak acceptance of the evils of the human condition a reflection of their own sense of moral impotence. It was the same with *one kind* of Existentialism. Americans were not attracted by the activist, ethically strenuous, and socially conscious emphasis in the writings of Jean-Paul Sartre. They found congenial, rather, Existentialism's analysis of the absurdities of life and the impossibility of unambiguous moral choices.

If we add to this religious and philosophical fatalism two further elements—the lack of major public debate on crucial issues, and the substantial reconciliation of intellectuals to the *status quo* (through comfortable jobs, research contracts, and the like)—we can begin to assess the full dimensions of the post-Hiroshima and post-McCarthy transformation. First came a deadening of sensibility. On this followed bewilderment and a feeling that problems had become too big and complex for the mere individual citizen to grasp (with both the national administration and the intellectuals aiding the process by insisting that only "experts" were qualified to express opinions). Finally ensued a *privatization* of life—a tendency on the part of each man to retreat to the cultivation of his own suburban garden. The vast majority of the accused in the McCarthy era had not the slightest desire to see their own woes made into test cases or matters of public concern. They ran for cover instead. Most cases of injustice never came to light and were correspondingly difficult to rectify after McCarthy's fall. This was still another reason why we had no Dreyfus Case.

In some moral dilemmas it is worse to be pettily right than nobly in error. Such could be said of countless Americans who in the course of becoming properly "sophisticated" about Communism lost their capacity for honest indignation. They forgot that every ideological commitment involves the risk of making a mistake, and that people who always play it safe make no contribution to awakening or enlightening their countrymen. Nor did the harm stop here. For a whole decade, school teachers and college professors denied their students the long-sanctioned right of the young to seek their own path and learn from their own errors. Most of the men and women who came of age in the decade 1948-1957—and who are now in their late twenties and early thirties—never knew what they were missing. Only a few of them were aware of their loss, and these I remember as bemused students, nostalgic for the ideological experiences that had passed them by.

Suddenly in the spring of 1960 I realized with a shock that a new student generation had sprung into life. In the widespread demonstrations against racial segregation, a new age group had won its political spurs. The picketings and meetings of that spring involved only a minority of college students. But this minority

was soon recognizable as the intellectually active and
devoted which in each generation take the moral lead.
And the fact that its energies subsequently turned toward activities on behalf of peace suggested that its
concern for racial equality formed part of a wider protest against inhumane behavior at home and abroad.[2]

To those of us who had grown discouraged by a
lack of response among our immediate juniors, the dis-
covery of this new student generation has been im-
mensely heartening. It has given us a chance to leap
over a ten-year span and take up again where we left
off when the ideological blight descended upon America.
In my own intellectual community of Greater Boston,
such efforts as the review *Dissent* and the neoradical
Committee of Correspondence have been notably reinforced by support from the very young.

Yet this support comes to us with a difference. We
who regard ourselves as stimulators of a New Left realize that our student allies do not think exactly as we
do. To them, we seem talky and old-fashioned. They
are impatient with words and with theories; they dislike
the vocabulary of leftist democracy which to my age
group is second nature. They prefer factual analysis—
and direct action where possible. Impatient with ideological rhetoric, they find almost incomprehensible the
pro-Communist and anti-Communist polemics that
shook the American left in the decades from 1917 to
1948.

Basically, I think this is a good thing. I find it healthy
that the students of today are starting off afresh with so
little concern for old ideological battles; in this sense

2. For a survey of student organizations and attitudes, see
Michael Harrington, "Notes on the Left," *The New Leader*,
XLIV (May 22, 1961), 15-18.

—as having wiped the slate clean—our country's ten-year slumber has been of positive benefit. I shall be quite happy to see the young people take leadership from us and direct the new radicalism of America into courses we would never have imagined. I agree that most of the traditional phraseology of the left has become worn and stale. I should welcome being treated as an old fogey if it should mean a new vigor and inspiration on the part of the young.

Yet in another sense it is too early for us to abdicate. The political virginity of today's students is wonderful —but it is also disconcerting. It is a curious experience for a person like myself, who has been accused of "softness" toward Soviet Russia, to find himself obliged to explain in the most elementary terms the differences between Communism and a free society. The experience of recent history is still relevant. The student generation of today can learn from the record of a yesterday that is fast sinking into legend or forgetfulness. It is for them primarily that I have dredged up the slime of an era that no one can recall without shame—in the hope that when *they* are confronted with their Dreyfus Case they will rise to the challenge better than we did in the years of our country's supreme moral crisis.

CHAPTER 12

The Present Imperative

THE MOST common and at the same time the most difficult question I have encountered in trying to present to audiences of students and young people my view of the present world emergency has not been a hostile one at all. It has been a friendly offer of help in the form of the query: "But what can I do *right now?*"

Of course there are all sorts of answers one can give. One can suggest wiring the President or buttonholing a couple of congressmen or—the advice most typical of our age of futile *expertise*—organizing a study group. In more militant vein, one can propose marching or sitting or picketing or trying to interfere with the launching of a nuclear submarine. But activities such as these are not for everybody: they suit the single-mindedly committed who are content simply to "bear witness" to their convictions. The more critical thinkers will probe further: they are looking for something tangible and practical, extending beyond individual protests on the part of tiny minorities. And to *their* questions it is hard to find satisfactory answers.

One way to begin is to suggest that the matter of war and peace cannot be dealt with in isolation from other issues. Indeed, the notion that this is possible is a further symptom of the contemporary American tendency to partition the continuous web of existence into neat specialties. Thus someone may function quite happily as an agitator for peace without feeling any obligation to concern himself with the state of the economy or of society as a whole, while an academic social scientist may pursue his researches for years without ever inquiring what the menace of war has to do with his scholarly conclusions. I trust the present essays have demonstrated how strenuously I dissent from such a view. They are an effort to show that our problems are all of a piece—that the character of our society at home (and that of other societies beyond our shores) bear a direct relation to the conduct of our foreign policy.

I have also implied that the ideological vacuum in the world today makes it peculiarly difficult to organize a coherent peace movement. Perhaps this needs a word of explanation. Just as Communism and capitalism are coming closer together on the common ground of welfare-state procedures, so the Western and the non-Western peoples are sharing the experience of a dissolution of ideology. I have tried to suggest the intellectual amorphousness of the characteristic leadership in the neutral and the underdeveloped nations. I have similarly pointed out that even in Western Europe— the seedbed of modern ideology and the area whose political tradition is most familiar to ourselves—democratic forms are losing their vitality and meaning. In the formerly colonial world there reigns a primitive nationalism narrowly focused on emergency requirements. In the West a dull uniformity underlies a deceptive variety of political labels. The ideologies known in Germany and Italy as Christian Democracy, in France as Gaullism, and in our own country as the bipartisan consensus display unmistakable features in common. They represent an ideology that denies ideology itself—and Utopia as well. In a formal sense they may be liberal and democratic, but in practice they erode the reality behind those forms. They are supported by no deep-running popular emotion. They rest, rather, on material prosperity, and beyond that, and more important than that, on weariness, on apathy, on passive acceptance, and on a tacit agreement not to discuss potentially "divisive" issues.

There remains the widespread sentiment grouped under the term "neutralism." Currently this is serving as the chief ideological bridge between the West and the newly liberated peoples, and nearly all the European socialists who have kept any breath of ideological fervor consider themselves neutralists in one or another form. In a non-Communist world that is almost without ideological conviction, neutralism offers the last reservoir of political commitment. But neutralism is scarcely even a faith; it is still farther from being a coherent set of political principles. Its convictions are usually stated in the negative—as a protest against the division of the world into two armed camps, or, still more uninspiringly, as the slogan of *ohne mich*—"leave me out of it." Neutralism as a faith and a way of life still needs to be defined. And I suspect that neither the Europeans (with their long experience of disillusionment) nor the Asians and Africans (with their intense absorption in developing their own economies) are in a position to do the job. Paradoxical as it may sound, this is a task to which Americans can properly turn their energies—American intellectuals, and more particularly the younger of them, who have not yet been worn down by the relentless compromises of life in a "consensus society."

And so to those who throw at me Lenin's classic question, "What is to be done?" I would answer that the first imperative is to revive the tradition of Utopia —to think through the meaning of the good society and in so doing to arrive at plans for preserving the possibility of its attainment.

At this point a note of undue solemnity threatens to intrude. American young people today are reluctant to commit themselves. The "cool" stance, the avoidance of naïveté at any price, the habit of suspending judgment until "all the facts are in"—a whole bundle of contemporary reticences, which any teacher of the young will recognize—generally suffice to quench their first flickers of ideological ardor. By far the greater part of our students find political commitment too strenuous for their taste; and they are suspicious of the emotionalism that deep personal involvement in a "cause" must entail.

Here, I think, the young people take the matter too hard by setting it up in terms of an all-or-nothing choice. They seem to be saying that if one cannot give oneself totally to a political faith, one had better not try at all: if full dedication is impossible, then detachment remains the only alternative. To me this is a false dichotomy. I believe there are a whole series of stages in commitment to an ideal, and that those who feel unable to give more than a part of themselves can still make a unique and valuable contribution. The experience of organized religion suggests that only a small portion of the faithful need embrace the life of the monastery.

In its simplest terms, commitment means no more

than establishing an order of priorities. With reference
to our present peril, it involves putting the physical
preservation of humanity ahead of loyalty to one's
nation or to any particular economic and social system.
It means a sense of shared dangers and shared aspirations transcending the military barriers that divide our
world.

Such a commitment—indeed, commitment of any
sort—is necessarily more emotional than intellectual.
Or, more precisely, the emotional and the intellectual
elements in it are so intimately bound together that
they can never be unraveled. That may be obvious
—a generation or two ago it would have been obvious
—yet in America today it is necessary to reiterate it,
since so many people seem to have gotten into their
heads the notion that there is something radically
wrong about emotion in ideology or politics. Perhaps
they equate it with fanaticism; our sufferings at the
hands of ideological fanatics over the past half-century
certainly offer reason enough for fearing partisan ex-
cesses. But that is not what I am speaking of. Fanaticism more often than not conceals a lack of true belief,
an inner void. I am thinking rather of the quiet,
deep-running conviction that gives purpose to a varied
and emotionally rich existence—a conviction that is
neither strident nor overbearing and relies more on
example than on exhortation.

No honest man of conviction has failed to undergo
the experience of having his beliefs shaken. At such
times he has found it necessary to go back to his emotional origins. In the case of a commitment to the
search for peace, a renewal of belief comes from a
few simple standards of humane behavior shared by
the religious and the atheists, and by the Western and

the non-Western peoples. These standards do not need to be defined: they define themselves in practice and in context as men of humane sentiments respond to individual crises in their public and private lives.

How such convictions are arrived at and held by large numbers of people remains for the most part a mystery. But one thing is certain: human beings do not reach moral and ideological positions by amassing quantities of "facts." In any given emergency, it is never possible—there is never time—to assemble all the relevant data. Today even more than in the past, both leaders and led have to make their decisions quickly and with inadequate information at their disposal. What is decisive is the response that has become habitual, the injunction or veto that speaks with the voice of the self-evident.

Compelling injunctions are necessarily simple. Indeed, the choices that confront us are far simpler than most Americans suppose. How often have I heard from my acquaintance the depressing refrain: "It is all too complicated!" Such an attitude has done untold harm in undermining a sense of public responsibility among our countrymen. In the respectable guise of intellectual scruple and suspended judgment, it has brought on nothing less than general moral abdication. When people say that the international situation is too complicated for them to understand, they really mean that it is too terrible for them to think about. They refuse to face it: their complaint of complexity is an elaborate evasion. And they are encouraged and justified in this attitude by the evasions of a national press that seems to find a perverse satisfaction in presenting the news in a partial, confused, and disjointed form.

The barest minimum of commitment, then, in facing the issues of peace and war might mean *doing* nothing at all; it might mean simply making the intellectual and moral effort required to understand the contemporary world, to unscramble reality from illusion, and humane behavior from brutality, in the colossal muddle of verbiage to which our leaders and our press subject us. Such an undertaking may sound modest—but under contemporary conditions it demands an act of energy and of will that may prove more taxing than any subsequent step along the path to ideological involvement.

Finally, I should say to those who are reluctant to commit themselves that dedication to an ideal—whether large or minimal—need in no sense be surrounded by an atmosphere of sternness or of gloom. On the contrary, it should be a source of vitality and joy. Most of us Americans today fancy ourselves given over to a hedonist ethic; that is just another aspect of the long-term change in our national character that has caught us by surprise in the last generation. But we take our pleasures sadly, or desperately, or mechanically. We have little delight in them because we find no meaning behind them. I wager that a great many Americans—particularly young Americans—are just waking up to this simple fact. And when they are fully awake, they will see that an existence without any concept of social transcendence is thin and empty, and that the pursuit of pleasure properly understood means a life suffused with the vision of a better world.

What do we need to do, then? There are two main types of nonconformist action today, both of which, I think, are largely futile. The first is an effort to "work on" the men in Washington, either by direct appeals to the President and his immediate advisers or, more commonly, by talking to some friend in the middle ranks of the administration. The trouble with this sort of activity is that it so soon becomes diluted and the persuaders so quickly lose their sense of proportion: a cordial word from someone in power, a minor verbal alteration in the draft of a public address—these come to rank as great victories in the ideological battle, and few people stop to notice how little has actually altered once the temporary effects of the gratifying incident have been absorbed.

The second type of pressure is that of the demonstration and the symbolic act. I do not wish to belittle the courage of the devoted people who invite derision and even jail sentences by publicly testifying to their beliefs. But here again as in the case of informal lobbying in Washington, the sense of proportion frequently gets lost. The agitators for peace are so caught up in their own doings that they fail to observe how small a part of the public responds to their appeal. They tend to become a confined circle of ideological associates, busily preaching to the converted and mistaking their limited and overlapping audiences for a mass movement.

Thus the real flaw in both kinds of "peace tactics" is a wearying sameness that the more critical-minded adherents of such movements are bound sooner or later to notice. And when they do, they become discouraged and drop out. One of the most difficult advisory assignments that has come my way is trying to sustain the flagging spirits of some militant for peace who, after throwing himself whole-heartedly into the cause and after suffering repeated disappointments, has suddenly decided he has had enough. "Didn't you know from the start," I feel like telling him, "that all but an infinitesimal portion of your activities would prove futile?" Or, more paradoxically, "If you had not given yourself so completely to your beliefs, you would not have become discouraged so quickly."

This, I think, is the biggest danger that threatens the American "peace movement" today. And I believe that those who strive for peace will not achieve clarity in their aims and methods until they have ceased to think in terms of short-run results. For two years now, the course of events has been going in a direction contrary to their hopes: since the spring of 1960, international misunderstanding has been on the increase, and the progress toward agreements that characterized the Eisenhower administration's middle years seems no more than a distant memory. Difficult days lie ahead; there are unmistakable danger signals of a revival of the hate-filled nationalism and anti-intellectualism that we associate with the McCarthy era. The peace people are going to suffer further disappointments; what they need is an organization—or better, an attitude—that will hold out over the long pull and that can stand repeated buffeting.

One idea which appeals to many of us is the establishment of a third political party. A new party would represent in tangible form our conviction that the problem of thermonuclear war is inseparable from the wider currents of politics and society, and that the attainment of international peace is dependent on a reinvigoration of the utopian tradition in domestic thought and action. We are well aware of the technical difficulties confronting any such effort. And the experience of the Progressive Party in 1948 warns us of how a ruthless minority can exploit a third-party movement to its own advantage—and to the ruin of the movement in question. But nearly a decade and a half have passed since then; the Communists are no longer even a minority force in American life. They would not have the remotest chance of perverting the aims of a new radical party as they did in the case of the party led by Henry Wallace fourteen years ago. Even with this disillusioning experience in our own past, some of us think we should like to try again.

A new political party, however, can be established only if the convictions that inspire it have *already* been created in the hearts of a significant minority of our fellow citizens. A mere federation of the existing peace organizations would not suffice—although it might be a first move in the proper direction. What we need, rather, as the prerequisite for future political action, is a loose alliance among like-minded people—a nationwide agreement on a few common principles, firmly held yet free from the sectarianism that limits the appeal of so many nonconformist groups today. The first principle would necessarily be negative. It would be a quiet but decisive refusal to go along with the majority—a personal withdrawal from the national consensus. This first step is also the hardest to take, since it entails a painful psychological rupture with the greater part of one's friends and associates. Yet once this initial obstacle is passed, the rest becomes clearer. Once individual Americans start thinking on their own —once they reject the "conventional wisdom" fed them by both political parties and the vast bulk of the press —then their minds leap on to all sorts of unsuspected corollaries and conclusions. They begin to see that the American economy as at present organized does not serve the common good as adequately as it is supposed to, and that our society is shot through with blind and destructive egoism.

Our first responsibility, then, is to dig in our toes and say "No." Our second is to locate the tens of thousands of our fellow citizens who actually feel as we do but have not yet found the moral and intellectual energy to think through the implications of their new beliefs. Our third is to link all these people together in a loose fellowship of thought and action and to spread the word farther and farther afield. Beyond that, however, there may be little we can do but wait. The majority of our countrymen will not change their minds in our favor from one day to the next. On the contrary, they are likely to regard us with increasing suspicion as the solidity of our purpose becomes ever more apparent. They will not turn to *us* for leadership and counsel until more decisive reverses in the international competition of ideologies have at last given overwhelming proof of the folly of our present national course.

In the meantime, we must keep up a drumfire of criticism and counterargument. We must ceaselessly oppose the official line—even when very few people seem to be listening. This function may sound tedious and unexciting—but it is basic to our whole cause and one that at the present time is being performed, against heartbreaking odds, by no more than a handful of liberal weeklies with small circulations and by the surprisingly influential newsletter of the Committee of Correspondence. Unless a steady reassurance through reasoned argument reaches the scattered bands of Americans whose nonconformist convictions are wavering and uncertain, they will lose hope and relapse into their former attitude of passive acceptance.

In brief, the future I envisage is what in the period

of Italy's resurgence was called a "conspiracy in open daylight"—a conspiracy, that is, in the sense of a minority actively concerting to achieve an ardently imagined end, but one carried on without secrecy and by men and women fully aware of their civic responsibilities. Or perhaps we might better call it a church in the catacombs. Like the early Christians, the Americans who think *otherwise* need not abandon their ordinary lives. But they must learn to remain steadfast in their beliefs while mingling with those who do not think as they do, and while engaging in practical pursuits that bear little relation to their ideal goals. This manner of life is not excessively difficult for people of only moderate courage to adopt. Yet at the very least it requires clearsightedness and an ability to withstand disappointment. It is for men and women who have been schooled in patience and know how to wait for a far from certain reward.

H. Stuart Hughes

H. STUART HUGHES was born in 1916 in New York City. He received his A.B. from Amherst College and his A.M. and Ph.D. from Harvard. Before World War II he also studied in Europe, at Heidelberg University and the University of Munich, and worked in the Archives Nationales in Paris.

Mr. Hughes taught history at Brown University before he enlisted in the Army as a private in 1941. By 1944 he was Chief of the Research and Analysis Branch of the Office of Strategic Services in the Mediterranean Theater; later he held the same post in Germany. He was relieved from active duty as a lieutenant colonel in 1946.

Since then he has been Chief of the State Department's Division of Research for Europe; Assistant Professor of History at Harvard; Associate Professor and Professor and head of the Department of History at Stanford; and, since 1957, Professor of History at Harvard, where he directs the interdepartmental program in History and Literature. He has also been a Visiting Member of the Institute for Advanced Study at Princeton, a Fellow of the Center for Advanced Study in the Behavioral Sciences at Stanford, a Fellow of the American Academy of Arts and Sciences, and the holder of a Guggenheim Fellowship.

Mr. Hughes is the author of five other books: *An Essay for Our Times* (1950); *Oswald Spengler: A Critical Estimate* (1952); *The United States and Italy* (1953); *Consciousness and Society* (1958); and *Contemporary Europe: A History* (1961). He also edited *Teachers of History: Essays in Honor of Laurence Bradford Packard* (1954). He lives in Cambridge, Massachusetts, with his wife and two children.

An active proponent of the movement against thermonuclear war, Mr. Hughes is a national sponsor of the Committee for a Sane Nuclear Policy and a founding member of the Committee of Correspondence.